GOD MADE *You* FOR MORE

DEVOTIONS & PRAYERS FOR TEEN GIRLS

JANICE THOMPSON

BARBOUR
PUBLISHING

© 2021 by Barbour Publishing, Inc.

Print ISBN 978-1-64352-949-3

All rights reserved. No part of this publication may be reproduced or transmitted for commercial purposes, except for brief quotations in printed reviews, without written permission of the publisher.

Churches and other noncommercial interests may reproduce portions of this book without the express written permission of Barbour Publishing, provided that the text does not exceed 500 words or 5 percent of the entire book, whichever is less, and that the text is not material quoted from another publisher. When reproducing text from this book, include the following credit line: "From *God Made You for More: Devotions and Prayers for Teen Girls*, published by Barbour Publishing, Inc. Used by permission."

Scripture quotations marked NIV are taken from the HOLY BIBLE, NEW INTERNATIONAL VERSION®. NIV®. Copyright © 1973, 1978, 1984, 2011 by Biblica, Inc.™ Used by permission. All rights reserved worldwide.

Scripture quotations marked KJV are taken from the King James Version of the Bible.

Scripture quotations marked NLV are taken from the New Life Version copyright © 1969 and 2003 by Barbour Publishing, Inc. All rights reserved.

Scripture quotations marked NLT are taken from the Holy Bible. New Living Translation copyright© 1996, 2004, 2015 by Tyndale House Foundation. Used by permission of Tyndale House Publishers, Inc. Carol Stream, Illinois 60188. All rights reserved.

Scripture quotations marked ESV are from The Holy Bible, English Standard Version®, copyright © 2001 by Crossway Bibles, a publishing ministry of Good News Publishers. Used by permission. All rights reserved.

Published by Barbour Publishing, Inc., 1810 Barbour Drive, Uhrichsville, Ohio 44683, www.barbourbooks.com

Our mission is to inspire the world with the life-changing message of the Bible.

Printed in China.

MADE FOR MORE

You were made for more. What comes to mind when you read those words? No doubt your first question is, "More of *what*?"

God created you in His image, and He has amazing things in store for your life—not just now, in your teen years, but as you get older. He wants to expand your thinking and increase your expectations so that you can catch a glimpse of what that will look like. To God, "more" is the norm. After all, He's the Creator of the entire universe! The whole world is in His hands, so "more" is no big deal to Him.

More *what*, you ask? More love. More peace. More joy. More godly friendships. More time with Him. More glimpses of heaven, even while you're still here on earth. All these things can be yours, along with a zillion other blessings, as long as you stick close to your loving heavenly Father.

No matter where you are in your journey—whether you're powering through a season of loneliness, heartache, disappointment, fear, insecurity, regret, shame, or unforgiveness, these 202 encouraging devotional readings will remind you that you—*yes, you!*—were made for so much more than any difficulty you might be facing.

Each reading includes a scripture and a prayer, guaranteed to lift your spirits and to remind you that "more" is God's heart for you. He has a marvelous plan for your life, one full of purpose and promise!

MORE LIKE HIM

Then God said, "Let us make man in our image, after our likeness. And let them have dominion over the fish of the sea and over the birds of the heavens and over the livestock and over all the earth and over every creeping thing that creeps on the earth." So God created man in his own image, in the image of God he created him; male and female he created them.
GENESIS 1:26–27 ESV

Remember, as a little girl, how you used to stare at two (supposedly) identical pictures, side by side, and try to find the differences? You had to look for a long time to see that one was truly different from the other, but after a while you started to notice teensy-tiny things that didn't match.

You were made to look so much like your Creator that people should have to squint and stare to find any differences. The way you love, the way you speak to others, the way you do your schoolwork. . .all these things should be a reflection of Him. You were made to be more like your heavenly Father in all areas of your life—from your thoughts to your relationships to your actions.

Does this mean God expects you to be perfect? No way! But keep on reflecting Him, girl, and you'll draw people to the One who truly is perfect. When you're more like Him, you make His heart very happy.

Lord, I want to draw people to You. May I be more like you every day. . .in every way. Amen.

MORE CONCERNED ABOUT THE INSIDE THAN THE OUTSIDE

"People look at the outward appearance, but the Lord looks at the heart."
1 Samuel 16:7 niv

Let's face it, every teen girl cares about her appearance. Her hair, her skin, her teeth, her clothes. . .these are the things most girls care very much about! But God created you to think bigger than that.

Take care of your body, of course. Keep your hair, skin, and teeth in tip-top shape. And have fun with your wardrobe choices. But on top of all that, spend time focusing on the inside. What's going on inside that heart of yours? Any bitterness or pain you need to get rid of? And what about your thought life? Are you spending too much time focusing on things you shouldn't?

The inside of you is as important as (if not more important than) the outside. It's true! God wants you to have an inside-out attitude from now on. When you live that way, the "more" lifestyle really can be yours!

It's not going to be easy, Lord. When I look in the mirror, I'm tempted to think about only the outside of me! But I know You want me to be more on the inside, so change my thinking, I pray. Amen.

MORE SEPARATION OF LIGHT FROM DARKNESS

*And God saw that the light was good.
And God separated the light from the darkness.*
GENESIS 1:4 ESV

"You can't straddle the fence, honey."

Sarah looked up into her mother's eyes. "Huh? What do you mean, Mom?"

"You need to make up your mind. You can't spend half your time hanging out with kids who are leading you down the wrong path and the other half saying you're a Christian. I'm not saying you should walk away from friendships, but I am saying that you need to back away from those kids a little so you don't start to look and sound like them. You want to be different from the rest of the pack."

Maybe you can relate to Sarah's struggle. You love hanging out with your friends, even the ones who are far from God. They're so much fun. Okay, maybe they do a lot of things they shouldn't, but you overlook that. "No judging" and all that. Right?

It's one thing to hang on to a friendship with someone who's in the dark, but it's another to start living like them! It's time to separate light from darkness, girl. How will you ever grow in your relationship with the Lord if you're caught up partying in the dark?

*Lord, the decision is made. I'm separating light
from darkness once and for all. I choose light! Amen.*

MORE FOCUSED ON OTHERS

*Do nothing from selfish ambition
or conceit, but in humility count
others more significant than yourselves.*
PHILIPPIANS 2:3 ESV

Mary Anne couldn't help the fact that she was born an only child. Was it her fault her parents had spoiled her rotten and given her everything she ever wanted? Sure, she turned out a little. . .demanding. But was that really her fault? From the time she was born, she was the center of their universe, after all.

Maybe you've known a few Mary Annes in your life. They always get what they want when they want it. And often they don't care who they have to step on to get it. They're bossy, rude, and demanding.

God didn't create you to be a queen, princess. Seriously. He created you to think more of others than yourself. If anyone's going to be the hero in your story, let it be those around you—the school lunch lady, for example. The bus driver. The delivery person. The doctor who works around the clock.

It's not all about you. It never was. Those words might sting, but they will also bring you life.

*Lord, I'm sorry for the times I've made
everything about me. I want to be more
outward focused from now on. Amen.*

MORE THAN REJECTED

No, God has not rejected his own people, whom he chose from the very beginning.
ROMANS 11:2 NLT

They don't want anything to do with you. You're not in their little clique. You're not invited to their parties. They don't even acknowledge you when you pass by them in the hallway at school.

And it hurts. . .a lot.

Being rejected stinks, especially when the rejection comes from people you'd like to be in relationship with. And sometimes it makes no sense at all!

Here's the truth—God made you for more than those feelings of rejection. Instead of asking, "Why doesn't anyone want me around?" change your focus. Say things like, "Thank You, God, that You created me for more. You have bigger, better plans for my relationships than that. And thank You for never rejecting me, Lord! You'll stick with me, no matter what."

When you live in His "more" lifestyle, you begin to see those rejections in perspective. And having His perspective is always a good thing.

Thank You for adjusting my perspective, Lord! I can see that You have better relationships ahead for me, and I'll be patient as I wait to see them happen. Amen.

MORE RIGHT THINGS

*Doing wrong leads to disgrace,
and scandalous behavior brings contempt.*
PROVERBS 18:3 NLT

You want to do the right thing. . .but it's so hard! The temptation to do the wrong thing always seems to win out, even though you don't want it to.

Need an example?

There's a big math test coming up. You know you should be studying, but your BFF invites you over to hang out. The next morning you wake up and realize you forgot to study. Ack! You take the test anyway. (What other choice do you have?) But you know you're in trouble. The questions seem impossible, a lot harder than you imagined.

Sure, you do your best, but when you get your grade, you find out you've made a D. Oh boy. Your parents are upset. Hey, you're upset with yourself too. You did set yourself up for failure, after all.

God made you to do the right thing in situations like these. Wrong choices always have consequences and leave you feeling like you should've tried harder. Next time, you can.

*You made me to do the right thing. It's on me, Lord!
I'm the one who has to choose, each and every day.
Help me make better choices, I pray. Amen.*

MORE HELP IN TIME OF TROUBLE

*God is our refuge and strength,
an ever-present help in trouble.*
Psalm 46:1 niv

Growing up, Jenna was the one giving help, not the one receiving. The oldest of six children, she was usually changing diapers, feeding one of the little ones, or trying to help her mom out with the meals. When she needed help with homework, she hardly ever got it. When she had a problem with a friend at school, she didn't have anyone to talk it over with.

Maybe you've been in Jenna's shoes. Maybe you're always the giver and rarely the receiver. There's good news for you today. God created you to receive help in times of trouble. Even when no one around you seems to notice what's going on, He does. He sees, He cares, and He's ready to intervene. So reach out to Him today. Watch as He pours out His abiding love and concern over your situation. And don't be surprised when He begins to move heaven and earth on your behalf. That's how much He adores you, after all!

*Thank You for being my Help in times
of trouble, Lord. You are my Refuge and
my Strength, and I'm so grateful! Amen.*

MORE SUPERSIZED DREAMS

And the Lord answered me: "Write the vision; make it plain on tablets, so he may run who reads it. For still the vision awaits its appointed time; it hastens to the end—it will not lie. If it seems slow, wait for it; it will surely come; it will not delay."
Habakkuk 2:2–3 esv

Sometimes when you order food at a fast-food restaurant, you hear: "Would you like to supersize that?" You probably say no because you know the extra calories wouldn't be good for you. But sometimes when life asks us that question, we should respond: "Yes! I'd like to supersize that!"

This is especially true when it comes to our dreams. Sometimes we dream too small. Think about the disciples after Jesus died and was resurrected. Do you think they ever imagined the impact they would have on the world, spreading the Gospel like wildfire? At some point, one or more of them had to cast the vision to do something larger than themselves.

Dreaming big doesn't mean we're necessarily following after our own dreams or ideas. No, to dream big means we pray, ask the Lord for His plans, and then catch the vision! Once the vision is "caught," we jump on board and run after it. Some of these dreams might seem too big to be realistic, but that's when we have to trust God. So get ready. When God is in it, the vision is out of this world!

*I want to dream bigger dreams, Lord.
You have great things planned for me!*

MORE GRACE

But he said to me, "My grace is sufficient for you, for my power is made perfect in weakness."
2 Corinthians 12:9 esv

Brianna was way too hard on herself. When she made a mistake, she chewed herself out. When she sang a song, it was never good enough. When she wrote a paper for school, she would question every single word. Her hair wasn't as cute as her friends', her body was too lumpy, and she didn't see herself as being pretty or likable.

In short, she beat herself up. When she was a little girl, her dad spoke ugly words over her. . .and they stuck, even though he divorced her mom and moved away. As a result, criticizing herself became a learned behavior. If he didn't think she was worthy of grace, she wouldn't either.

And it didn't stop there. Brianna had a hard time giving grace to others as well. She couldn't seem to help herself.

Maybe Brianna's story is hitting a nerve. Maybe it's a little too close to home. You were made to receive and give more and more grace. So don't beat yourself up, girl! God created you for more than that!

I will do my best not to be so hard on myself, Lord, but I'm going to need Your help. Amen.

MORE WILLING TO WORK

Whatever you do, work at it with all your heart, as working for the Lord, not for human masters.
Colossians 3:23 niv

Remember the old Disney movie *Snow White*? She stumbles into the world of the seven dwarfs, who seem to be nothing short of workaholics. Every morning they head off to work, singing a merry tune to prepare them for the day ahead.

Do you head off to school each morning with a song in your heart too? The same joy that made the dwarfs want to work should give you energy for the tasks you face, girl.

Not feeling it? No worries! Just turn on a worship song and sing your heart out as you get dressed for school. "Hi-ho! Hi-ho! Your heart is changing so! The more you worship, the better you feel, hi-ho, hi-ho!"

You were created to do good work, and it's important to dive right in. God isn't looking for a lazybones. Only the finest for the work at hand! So get to it. Hi-ho, girl!

Lord, I don't always show You my hi-ho attitude, but here I go! Thank You for giving me the desire to work hard and do my best, Father. Amen.

MORE COURAGEOUS

"Have I not commanded you? Be strong and courageous. Do not be afraid; do not be discouraged, for the LORD your God will be with you wherever you go."
JOSHUA 1:9 NIV

"Me? Brave?" Trina laughed. "Um, no. I'm the least brave person I know."

"Trina, you need to stop saying that." Her best friend, Chelsea, clucked her tongue. "You've been through some really hard things these past couple of years, and you still have your faith. I'd say you're one of the bravest girls I've ever known."

Trina still wasn't sure. Right now, she didn't feel so brave. Her knees were knocking, her hands were trembling, and her "want-to" was fading.

Maybe you've been there. You need the courage to accomplish something big. Or maybe it's not even big. Maybe it's just a certain task at school you've been dreading. You don't have the courage to tackle it, but guess who does? The same God who raised Jesus from the dead wants to help you with your situation. He also wants to give you courage in the moment when you feel your weakest.

You were made for more courage, girl. More and more and more. So stand up straight and tall! Don't let those wobbly knees worry you. God's got this. And with His hand in yours, you've got it too.

I'm done talking about how cowardly I am, Lord! I'll speak brave words over my situation today. With Your help, I've got this. Amen.

MORE THAN YOUR PAIN

*For I consider that the sufferings of this
present time are not worth comparing
with the glory that is to be revealed to us.*
ROMANS 8:18 ESV

Mia groaned as she rolled over in bed. For months, the painful monthly cramps were more than she could handle. She tried everything the doctor suggested—over-the-counter pain meds, breathing techniques, warm showers, even essential oils. Nothing seemed to ease the ongoing pain. On days like this, when she struggled to think straight, Mia wondered if she would ever be more than her pain.

Perhaps you're walking through a similar season. The pain grips you and whispers in your ear, "You're mine. I'm holding you captive! You'll never escape me."

Here's the truth about pain: God is bigger. He's bigger than your diagnosis. He's bigger than the meds. He's bigger than the situation. And He loves you. . .bigger. His love for you goes above and beyond the horrible pain you're facing now.

He's more than your pain. And He wants to ease your burdens—physical and emotional. Don't give in to defeat. Don't listen to the voice of the enemy as he whispers, "Normal life is behind you." It's not. God wants to prove that to you, so don't give up.

*Lord, I give the pain to You.
I put my trust in You, Jesus. Amen.*

MORE KINDNESS TOWARD OTHERS

*Be kind to one another, tenderhearted,
forgiving one another, as God in Christ forgave you.*
EPHESIANS 4:32 ESV

"Is being kind really so hard, RaeLyn?"

The third grader looked up into her mother's eyes. It was harder than Mom knew, especially when her older brother was so mean all the time. But instead of arguing, she just sighed and did as she was told.

Maybe you've had a hard time being kind to the meanies in your life. That girl down the street who's so pushy. That friend who insists she knows more about everything than you do. That teacher who always has something not so nice to say about the work you turn in.

Not everyone is easy to treat kindly, but that doesn't mean you shouldn't try. God created you to be kind to everyone, not just the people who make it easy.

So who's on your radar today? Who's been making life difficult? Take the kindness challenge. Go out of your way to show kindness to the very person who (in your opinion) least deserves it. Then watch and see what the Lord does.

*It's not going to be easy, Lord,
but I'll be kind, even to the ones who've
hurt me. I trust You in this, Father. Amen.*

MORE TESTIFYING

"Very truly I tell you, we speak of what we know, and we testify to what we have seen, but still you people do not accept our testimony."
JOHN 3:11 NIV

Have you ever gotten super excited about a product (or sports team)? Maybe you couldn't wait to sing its praises for all to hear. You went around talking about it with glowing reviews in the hopes that others would catch on.

You were designed to testify! That desire to "spread the good news" is inside of you for a reason. God placed it there and plans for you to be as excited about sharing the good news of the Gospel as you are about last night's game.

The next time you're wondering how to go about sharing the Gospel, don't forget how fun and easy it was to share that last bit of good news about your favorite restaurant, candy bar, or shampoo. Surely if you can sing the praises of those things, you can share what God has done to change your life.

Lord, give me the right words to say—whether I'm hanging out with a close friend or sharing a post online. I want to testify to Your goodness! Amen.

MORE OVERCOMING

"I have told you these things, so that in me you may have peace. In this world you will have trouble. But take heart! I have overcome the world."
JOHN 16:33 NIV

Emma wasn't much for fighting. If someone came up against her—wanting to start an argument—she rarely stated her case. She just backed down. The same could be said of her struggles with temptation. She didn't feel like fighting, so she just gave in to the temptation to eat those sugary foods, even though her dentist advised against it.

Emma didn't see herself as an overcomer. She pictured herself as a loser, which made giving in even easier.

Maybe you can relate. It's easier not to fight. It's easier to just sigh and give in. But God designed you to be an overcomer. He doesn't want you to tuck your tail between your legs and give up without a fight. Keep going, girl! Lift that head and keep marching, even when the enemy threatens. You will overcome with Jesus' help!

I was made to overcome, Lord. I'm not giving in. No way, nohow! In You I will take heart. Amen.

MORE SELF-CONTROL

But the fruit of the Spirit is love, joy, peace, patience, kindness, goodness, faithfulness, gentleness, self-control; against such things there is no law.
GALATIANS 5:22–23 ESV

"I can say no to that."

Alyssa stood in front of the open freezer door, staring at the carton of ice cream inside. It seemed to call out to her, like a lighthouse leading her safely onward. Oh, how she wanted it. She could almost taste the yummy chocolate chips now.

"No." She shook her head as she closed the freezer door. "I'm saying no to that. I don't need the calories or the sugar! It's bad for my teeth and my waistline!"

Saying no isn't easy, but sometimes it's the best thing we can do. And before you say, "Oh, man! I have such a hard time saying no—to food, to people, to temptation," hold up a minute. You are empowered by the King of all kings! He's given you His Spirit and all the gifts attached. Self-control is one of those gifts!

You were made to exhibit more self-control, whether you think you can or not.

Oh, and by the way. . .you can! (And you should!)

Lord, thank You for the reminder that I can do all things through You. . .even say no! Thanks for giving me self-control. Amen.

MORE OVERFLOWING

You prepare a table before me in the presence of my enemies; you anoint my head with oil; my cup overflows.
PSALM 23:5 ESV

"Surprise!"

Katie looked around the room, completely shocked. A surprise birthday party. . .for her? Off in the distance she saw her best friend from third grade. What in the world? And her neighbor from the old neighborhood? How had they pulled this off without her knowing? She glanced at her mom and smiled. She had done all of this. And Katie was tickled pink! Her heart was absolutely overflowing with gratitude and love. And judging from the broad smiles on their faces, everyone else was delighted too.

Maybe you've felt that way at times. You've been so overwhelmed (in a good way) that your heart seemed to burst with joy. The overflow spilled onto everyone you came in contact with. Talk about a joy encounter!

God designed you for more of those, girl! When it comes to blessings, He loves to surprise His kids. So keep your eyes open! He's sure to delight you with even more.

Lord, my heart is full to overflowing, thanks to You and Your many blessings. How can I ever thank You, Father? My cup overflows! Amen.

MORE POWERFUL PRAYERS

Therefore confess your sins to each other and pray for each other so that you may be healed. The prayer of a righteous person is powerful and effective.
JAMES 5:16 NIV

You know what it's like to have a quick chat with a friend, don't you, girl? Maybe you pass her in the hallway at school and say hello. It's fun, but hanging out with a friend for an hour or two is better, especially if she lets you spill your guts.

Jesus is a "spill your guts" kind of friend. He wants more time with you. And He doesn't just want you to say the usual "Bless my family" prayers. He wants you to get to the deep stuff, like how you're feeling after you failed that test or what made you snap at your mom yesterday morning as you left for school. He wants to listen to all of it and then respond, wrapping His arms of love around you in the process.

He made you to be a powerful prayer warrior, even when you're young. God created you to communicate with Him. So don't just scratch the surface. Go deep with Him, girl!

Lord, sometimes I feel like I need Your guidance to know how to pray effectively. Teach me how to pray so that I can go deep with You. Amen.

MORE AFFECTION FOR OTHERS

*And godliness with brotherly affection,
and brotherly affection with love.*
2 PETER 1:7 ESV

Olivia was super-duper affectionate and loving. She seemed to know just how to share kindness and affection with others. Whenever someone was hurting—after the loss of a child, for instance, or the death of a parent—she seemed to know the right words to say to make them feel like they weren't alone. She just had a knack.

Not everyone has that gift, but it's one we all should work on. God calls us to show more brotherly affection—more love and caring—not just for those in pain or need, but in general.

So how are you doing in the "affection" department? Don't panic! This isn't a "hug 'em until they give up" kind of affection we're going for here, though hugs are nice. Affection can be shown with a greeting card, a text message, a hot meal, or a tray of fresh-baked cookies. However you choose to show it, God will honor it. So what are you waiting for? Find someone who needs affection today!

*I'll do it, Lord! I'll look for someone who's in need
of brotherly affection, and I'll pour it out in
whatever way You choose. Amen.*

MORE HARMONY

Live in harmony with one another. Do not be proud, but be willing to associate with people of low position. Do not be conceited.
ROMANS 12:16 NIV

Meredith was happy to attend her kid sister's choir concert. . .until she got there. Unfortunately, the seventh-grade girls' choir was a little off pitch. Okay, more than a little. They were just plain awful.

Meredith, who was a pretty good musician, thought she might lose her mind as several of the sopranos screeched out a note that didn't even come close to the one they were aiming for. The whole thing felt like fingernails down a chalkboard. Eek!

Harmony is lovely. . .but only when it works. If the sopranos, altos, tenors, and basses don't sing in the same key, the song is destroyed.

The same is true when relationships aren't harmonious. When people begin to squabble or cause unnecessary noise, the whole dynamic can change (and not for the better). God never intended for us to fall out of harmony with friends, family members, or loved ones. He longs for us to love the way He loves and for harmony to flow. So tuck away any pride, and do your best to get along with others, girl! No fingernails down the chalkboard for you!

Lord, I want harmonious relationships. Thank You for showing me that harmony is possible, even with difficult people. Amen.

MORE SHINING LIKE THE SUN

"Then the righteous will shine like the sun in the kingdom of their Father. Whoever has ears, let them hear."
MATTHEW 13:43 NIV

Remember that song you used to sing as a kid, about not hiding your light under a bushel? You were born to let the light of God shine bright—in your actions, your words, and your attitude.

Maybe you hear that and say, "Yeah, but you don't know the icky stuff I'm walking through right now. How can I possibly shine my light with all this stuff going on? There's just no way."

People are watching. . .right now. They want hope. They're waiting for someone in the valley to pipe up and say, "Hey, guys! I'm here too, but I'm not giving up on Jesus! I'm not letting go of my faith."

Be the light. Shine the light. Don't be afraid to speak up, even in the hard times. So what if you slip up one day and come back shining the next? They won't see you as a hypocrite. You'll just look like what you are—human.

Lord, I want to shine like the sun! I'll mess up from time to time and accidentally let my light go out. But I'll be back in the light in no time, with Your help, Father. Amen.

MORE CARING FOR THOSE IN NEED

*Do nothing out of selfish ambition or vain conceit.
Rather, in humility value others above yourselves,
not looking to your own interests but each
of you to the interests of the others.*
PHILIPPIANS 2:3–4 NIV

Madison couldn't help herself. Her heart went out to those less fortunate, and she had to help. The homeless man at the busy intersection? She asked her mom to keep bottled water and pop-top cans of tuna in the car for him. The local women's shelter? Every Thanksgiving she talked her parents into helping serve food. Her church's food pantry? Madison simply couldn't stand the idea that people in unfortunate situations wouldn't receive the things they needed.

Maybe you're a little bit like Madison. Your heart breaks to see people in genuine need. Maybe you're the one buying Christmas gifts for underprivileged children or baking pumpkin pies for the shelter's holiday gathering.

God created you to care about those less fortunate. Every ounce of passion that's stirring inside of you toward them is straight from His heart. So do what you can, girl! Look after the needs of others, and you'll never go wrong.

*Lord, thank You for the reminder that You created
me to care about those less fortunate than myself.
I want to do all I can, Father. With Your help,
I can make a difference. Amen.*

MORE CHANCES TO LIVE OUT YOUR LOVE FOR GOD

Whoever claims to love God yet hates a brother or sister is a liar. For whoever does not love their brother and sister, whom they have seen, cannot love God, whom they have not seen.
1 John 4:20 niv

"Do as I say, not as I do." How many times have you felt like saying that? You want to lead your friends by example but fail miserably at times. (Hey, at least you're not alone! We all fail miserably at times, so you're in good company!)

Aren't you glad God doesn't give up on you, even when you're ready to give up on yourself? He gives you chance after chance to live out your love for Him, even after the really big mess-ups. No, you won't always get it right, but when you do, it feels really good. And it's a great reflection of Him for all who are watching.

You'll have plenty of chances ahead to lead by example, so don't spend too much time worrying about the past. Just keep your eyes on Him and keep moving forward.

I want to be a good example for others, Lord, a light that shines in the darkness. I confess, I've often messed up and been a "Don't let this happen to you" example instead. But I'll keep moving ahead. Thanks to Your wonderful forgiveness, I have plenty of chances to get this right. Amen.

MORE PATIENCE

*Love is patient, love is kind. It does not envy,
it does not boast, it is not proud. It does not
dishonor others, it is not self-seeking, it is not
easily angered, it keeps no record of wrongs.*
1 CORINTHIANS 13:4–5 NIV

You were created to be more patient.

Ouch. Maybe those words cause a fluttering of pain in your heart. You don't *want* to be more patient, thank you very much. You've been patient enough already—with your parents, with stuff going on at school, with the never-ending problems with your best friend. How could the Lord possibly expect you to be even more patient? That hardly seems fair.

But wait. Hasn't He been patient with you? Wasn't He right there loving you, even when you turned your back on Him and tried to walk away? God wants you to learn from His example, to experience (and show) that sort of patience with all the people you come in contact with.

Yes, even the ones you struggle with.

Especially the ones you struggle with.

*Lord, patience doesn't come naturally to me.
But I know I can have more of it with Your help.
Show me how to be more patient so that I
can be more like You, Father. Amen.*

MORE GOOD PLANS

*Many are the plans in a person's heart,
but it is the L<small>ORD</small>'s purpose that prevails.*
P<small>ROVERBS</small> 19:21 NIV

What a busy girl you are! You have plans, plans, and more plans. Your calendar is so full it's about to burst! You have school, family stuff, vacations, sports, friends to hang out with, church stuff, and tests. . .lots and lots of tests. When you look ahead to the future, you've got colleges to think about, jobs to find, and maybe even a little romance! Whew! It's a lot!

Don't you love today's scripture? When you're overwhelmed with *your* plans, the Bible reminds you that *His* purposes are the ones that win out, no matter how many plans you have. Even if you're running a hundred miles an hour, He still wins the race.

God created you to make good plans, so make sure everything you're doing is really His best for you. If not, then ask Him to rearrange your plans, making them *His* plans.

*My plans are fun, Lord, but sometimes
a little overwhelming! Help me follow
Your plans, I pray. Amen.*

MORE GOOD AND PERFECT GIFTS

Every good gift and every perfect gift is from above, coming down from the Father of lights, with whom there is no variation or shadow due to change.
JAMES 1:17 ESV

All her life, Kassy's mom would say, "Honey, I just want the best for you."

Kassy did her best not to groan out loud, especially in front of her parents, but she knew what that meant, of course. Mom disagreed with her current choices and wanted something better for her than what she had chosen for herself. (Why did Mom always have to be right?)

God wants "better" for you as well. No matter how many precious gifts life throws your way, His are bigger, better, holier. So don't try to outdo Him! Don't ever think, *Hey, I know what's best for me, so I'll take it from here, God.*

The truth is, only *He* knows what's best, and He's already planning to dish it out. So don't waste your time attempting to be smarter than your loving heavenly Father. He is, after all, the Giver of all good gifts! (And boy, does He want to give them to you today!)

You give good gifts, Lord, better than anything I could come up with for myself. Thank You for showering me with love. Amen.

MORE REAL

For our boast is this, the testimony of our conscience, that we behaved in the world with simplicity and godly sincerity, not by earthly wisdom but by the grace of God, and supremely so toward you.
2 CORINTHIANS 1:12 ESV

"She's such a fake. You can see right through her."

Victoria wished she hadn't overheard her so-called friend talk about her behind her back, but what could she do about it now? Did her friends really see her as a fake? Was she?

Okay, so she tried a little too hard. And yes, she laughed too loud, tried to be the center of attention whenever possible. But Victoria thought all those things would make people like her more, not turn them away.

Maybe you've been there. You've been accused of not being the real deal. Or maybe you have a friend who spends too much time faking it.

God designed you to be authentically you. No one else. Nothing put on. Nothing over the top. Just. . .you. So relax. Be yourself. Don't be afraid to let your guard down and allow people to get to know you—the *real* you.

Lord, I want to be authentic, not just in Your sight but in the sight of others. I need Your help to let go of the fakeness, Father. Amen.

MORE GRACE AND TRUTH

*For the law was given through Moses;
grace and truth came through Jesus Christ.*
JOHN 1:17 ESV

Maybe you've heard the expression "Speak the truth in love."

It's harder than it sounds, isn't it? What if the truth you need to speak is a *hard* truth? Your friend is asking your opinion about a task she performed poorly. Do you lie? Or do you go for it, saying something like, "Well, it wasn't your best moment"?

Grace and truth came through Jesus. You might read those words and think, *What does this have to do with my friend?* Everything. He supernaturally gives you the ability to share the truth in His love. Think about this: when your mom has to confront you after you've messed up, she needs grace to do so. The same is true with you! He'll give you grace when you need it too. And He can show you how to give it in a loving way.

Grace and truth work hand in hand. They were never meant to operate apart from each other. And Jesus Christ—the same One who offered you eternal life—offers you a way to merge grace and truth when dealing with those around you. You were made to do it, girl!

You've given me grace for today, Lord, and I plan to use it as needed! Thank You for sharing it with me. May I learn to share it with others! Amen.

MORE TREASURES IN HEAVEN

"Sell your possessions, and give to the needy. Provide yourselves with moneybags that do not grow old, with a treasure in the heavens that does not fail, where no thief approaches and no moth destroys. For where your treasure is, there will your heart be also."
Luke 12:33–34 esv

Commercials make a big deal out of having more, more, more. Magazines say you can't live without the latest, greatest clothes, shoes, electronics, and so on. They tell you that you were made for more. But more of what? Money? Expensive phones and cars? If we believed the ads out there, we were meant to have a zillion dollars in the bank!

The treasures that this world has to offer are lovely, to be sure. Nice cars, fancy houses, expensive clothes, and jewelry—these things are terrific when they come our way. But they are not our true treasures.

The Bible teaches us that our treasures are laid up for us in heaven. Down here—on earth—we can't chase after material things. When we do have more than enough, God instructs us to remember the needy among us and to make provision for them.

Your treasure is coming, girl. But it might not look like a new laptop or a pair of shoes!

Lord, You have treasures waiting for me in heaven. I can't wait to see them! But for now I'm okay without a big castle down here, I promise! Amen.

MORE GOOD WORKS

"Truly, truly, I say to you, whoever believes in me will also do the works that I do; and greater works than these will he do, because I am going to the Father."
JOHN 14:12 ESV

When we're little we say things like, "I want to do amazing things for You, Lord! Send me to Africa! Send me to India! I'm going to change the world one day."

Maybe you're secretly wondering if you'll ever do anything truly awesome for the Lord. Oh, you talked your mom into sponsoring that child in a third-world country, sure. And you helped her put together Christmas boxes for kids in need. Yes, you bring canned goods to your church's food pantry. . .but will you ever do anything big?

Girl, you're doing big things now! Every day you pour into the lives of people around you. You minister to broken hearts by listening, you meet needs by giving, you're a good student, and you pray, pray, pray. That's the very best gift of all.

You were created for "more/greater" works, so there will be more exciting adventures ahead. But until then, don't beat yourself up. You're doing amazing things for the kingdom of God!

*Thanks for trusting me with
greater works, Lord! Amen.*

MORE SPIRIT FRUIT

But the fruit of the Spirit is love, joy, peace, patience, kindness, goodness, faithfulness, gentleness, self-control; against such things there is no law.
GALATIANS 5:22–23 ESV

Do you ever look at the list of the fruits of the Spirit and say, "Lord, do I really have to live out *all* of them. . .at the very same time? I mean, it's hard enough to be patient, but if You throw in self-control at the same time, it's just too much."

It *is* difficult to be good all the time, isn't it? To be kind, loving, joy filled, patient, and faithful? That hardly leaves time for hissy fits or temper tantrums. But God created you to exhibit more fruit—all at once and all the time. No, it's not easy. Yes, you will mess up. But God loves every step you take in the right direction.

Take a look at the list of fruits. Is there one you struggle with more than the others? Does your patience wear thin? Do you have trouble remaining faithful? Give that fruit to God and then watch as He reactivates it, making it a thing of beauty.

Lord, I give this fruit basket to You! You know my weaknesses and strengths. Help me where I'm failing, and make me as fruity as You've called me to be. Amen.

MORE THAN OUR UNFORGIVENESS

"For if you forgive others their trespasses, your heavenly Father will also forgive you, but if you do not forgive others their trespasses, neither will your Father forgive your trespasses."
MATTHEW 6:14–15 ESV

You've tried to forgive. You've paced the floor, begging God to help you let it go. You've written letters to release the person from the pain they've caused but then didn't send them. There's a part of you that wants to cling to the hurt. For whatever reason, you can't seem to let it go. And yet it's eating you alive. Life on the other side of it would be so much better.

If only. . .

You were made to forgive. It's that simple (and that difficult). God forgives you and expects you to forgive others. Have you been badly hurt? Yes. Is that person apologetic or feeling even a little bit guilty? Probably not. Does that mean you have the satisfaction of holding him (or her) in unforgiveness forever?

No.

You have to forgive. It's not a suggestion; it's a principle that will save your life because it will release you from the demons of bitterness. When that happens, the one who is set free is not your adversary. It's you.

Lord, today I choose to forgive the one who has hurt me, once and for all. Show me how, I pray. Amen.

MORE OF HIM

I want to know Him. I want to have the same power in my life that raised Jesus from the dead. I want to understand and have a share in His sufferings and be like Christ in His death.
Philippians 3:10 NLV

Imagine someone gives you a puzzle to work but there's no lid to the box. Hard, right? You don't know what the final picture is going to look like. You're only able to piece together one little section at a time with no understanding of the finished product.

In some ways, following the Lord is like that. You know He's good. You're sure He loves You. But you don't see "all" of Him. He's revealing Himself to you in snippets—one tiny puzzle piece at a time. As the segments of the story come into focus, you're more convinced than ever that He's in charge and cares for you. But even then, you don't have a full understanding.

Isn't it wonderful to know that heaven will provide all the answers you're seeking? And you don't have to wait until then to know Him better. The Word of God says that you can know God even now—not just in the power of His resurrection but when you're going through suffering. No matter what you're walking through, He longs to reveal more of Himself.

Lord, I want to know You more. I was created to be intimately acquainted with You. Amen.

MORE HONESTY

*A false witness will not go unpunished,
and whoever pours out lies will not go free.*
PROVERBS 19:5 NIV

When you were little, what did you say you wanted to be when you grew up? Some people say, "I want to be a doctor," or "I want to be a marine biologist." One thing you never hear is this: "I think I'll be a liar when I grow up." (Hey, it's just not something most people aspire to!)

God created you to live a life of honesty, girl. Sure, it's hard. You try to avoid those little white lies, but every now and again they slip out. You just can't seem to help yourself. Warning: don't ever get comfortable with those occasional slipups, or lying will soon become a habit!

The Bible has a lot to say about lying, but let's cut to the chase: God is not a fan. If you check out today's verse, you'll see just how He feels about it. A false witness (a liar) will not go unpunished.

Yikes! If you lie, there will be a price to pay. . .and that's the truth!

You made me for honesty, Lord. I don't want lying to become a habit. But I need Your help with this one, God! Make me completely honest, I pray. Amen.

MORE THAN YOUR MESS-UPS

*If we confess our sins, he is faithful and
just to forgive us our sins and to cleanse
us from all unrighteousness.*
1 John 1:9 esv

Chloe got the shivers every time she remembered how she'd spoken to her best friend on the day of their big fight. Audrey hadn't spoken to her since that horrible day, and Chloe didn't really blame her. Who blew up like that and said such cruel things to a good friend? Ugh. Could she ever make things right now? Or would things always be the same as they were now—just plain ugly?

Maybe you've blown up in the same way. You've spoken to a parent, a sibling, a teacher, or a friend in a way that you regret. It was out of character for you, but now everyone sees you as some sort of beast.

God can take a situation—even one as rough as yours—and mend it. Extend a hand of apology. Speak the twelve words that can heal a relationship: "I am sorry. I was wrong. Please forgive me. I love you." Then watch as God makes your regrets a thing of the past.

*Jesus, I don't know how You can fix the
situations that seem unfixable, but I
place them in Your hands today. Amen.*

MORE OF A GOOD SPORT

*Have this mind among yourselves,
which is yours in Christ Jesus.*
PHILIPPIANS 2:5 ESV

You've seen them in action—those girls who are bad sports. They lose a softball game but make a big deal out of how the umpire robbed them. They come in second in a race but insist they should have been first.

Everyone wants to be a winner. Everyone wants to take home the big prize. But the bigger prize is the one you'll take home (in your heart) if you're a good sport. That's part of the "more" lifestyle, in fact—admitting that you're not always going to be the top dog.

What does it mean to be a good sport? First, congratulate the one with the blue ribbon, and mean it. Second, don't make a big deal out of the times you feel you've been cheated. There will be plenty more times when you're shown favor. Third, leave the outcome in God's hands. It's just a game, after all. . .something that is noneternal. You're on the playing field to learn, so learn the best lesson of all: be a good sport.

*Lord, I need to adjust my attitude
both on and off the field sometimes.
I'll need Your help, God! Amen.*

MORE THAN YOUR DISAPPOINTMENTS

Do not be anxious about anything, but in everything by prayer and supplication with thanksgiving let your requests be made known to God. And the peace of God, which surpasses all understanding, will guard your hearts and your minds in Christ Jesus.
Philippians 4:6–7 esv

You feel like you've been waiting forever and finally got your answer. Ugh! It's not the one you were hoping for. You didn't get the part in the play you were anticipating. You're disappointed, as anyone would be. Why didn't the director pick you? Your audition was great. . .right? And why did he stick you in the chorus? Didn't he see your talents and abilities were better than that?

Now what? Where do you go with that broken heart of yours? Do you give up altogether or try something new?

Disappointments come no matter how much you wish them away. But you can take those disappointments to your heavenly Father and ask for His perspective. Perhaps He has a better part in a future play. Or maybe He has a completely different project in mind for you. Ultimately, He has a terrific plan in place for you, and you can trust Him with the details.

Lord, I don't understand. . .but I do choose to trust. I'm more than my disappointments, Father. Thank You for bringing hope. Amen.

MORE PURITY

Don't let anyone look down on you because you are young, but set an example for the believers in speech, in conduct, in love, in faith and in purity.
1 TIMOTHY 4:12 NIV

When you hear someone say the word *purity*, what do you think of? A bride on her wedding day, dressed in white? A tiny child, laughing and cooing?

If you look up the word in the dictionary, you'll find a variety of meanings, including "free from contamination" or "free from immorality." To be pure means you're undefiled. Untouched. Completely spotless and clean.

God made you for purity. If that sounds impossible, you're right. . .it is. The only way you can ever truly be pure (in your thoughts, your heart, and your actions) is to allow Jesus to cleanse you from your mess-ups. You can try your hardest to stay pure (and you should), but when it comes to super-duper scrubbing bubbles to wash away your sin, only God can handle that.

The Lord wants you to value purity, though, so work on it. Pure thoughts. Pure actions. Pure convictions. All of these are possible when you say, "Jesus, I want to be more like You!"

*Lord, help me with my purity, I pray.
I want to be clean inside and out. Amen.*

MORE INTEGRITY

The integrity of the upright guides them, but the crookedness of the treacherous destroys them.
Proverbs 11:3 esv

Do you consider yourself to be a girl of integrity (honesty and righteousness)? Do you have strong morals (solid beliefs in what's right and what's wrong)? Are you honest? Do you speak the truth?

These days, not a lot of people have integrity. Many give in to temptation and do the wrong thing when no one's looking. But God wants more than that for you, girl! He wants you to be upright (righteous), even when no one can see what you're up to.

How do you make sure you're walking in integrity? Stick close to Jesus. Follow Him instead of following your friends. When you mess up, turn around and go the other way. Admit when you've done something wrong. Make it right. Be a girl who does what she says she's going to do.

Having integrity takes work. It's not easy. But it's so worth it. You are a representative of Jesus Christ on this planet, after all, and want to make Him look good. So do your best. . .and trust Him with the rest.

*Lord, I'll do my best to be a girl of integrity.
I want to represent You well! Amen.*

MORE STYLE

*[Be] hospitable, a lover of good,
self-controlled, upright, holy, and disciplined.*
TITUS 1:8 ESV

Jilli was a girl with a lot of style. Her hair always looked great. She knew how to pick out the most put-together outfits, right down to the perfect earrings. Friends always commented on how nice she looked. This "style" spilled over into her life as well. She was known for being kind and treating people with grace.

All of God's girls have a certain style, a particular way of doing things. That's how God created you, to be stylish for Him. But what does this have to do with our spiritual walk? We're representing Jesus, so we don't want to turn up in public looking like a mess. Well, not all the time, anyway. But more importantly, we want to be inviting. Our "style" shouldn't turn people away. It should draw them to us.

Jesus had His own style too. He wasn't handsome (according to the Bible), but people couldn't wait to hang out with Him. This had nothing to do with His clothing, to be sure. It had everything to do with His compassion and love for others. His "style show" went far beyond the physical and served as an invitation to others to draw near and to sit at His feet and learn. To love and be loved.

Put on a Jesus style show today, girl!

*Lord, I want to be like You.
May Your style be my style. Amen.*

MORE TRUST, LESS ANXIETY

*Cast all your anxiety on him
because he cares for you.*
1 PETER 5:7 NIV

"Kylie, can I ask you a question?"

"Sure." Kylie looked up from her homework into her friend's eyes. "What's up?"

"I'm just getting a little worried about you," Emery explained. "You've been working round the clock and you're always so. . .stressed out. Anxious."

"I've got to get this paper finished for my history class. And after that I've got to study for my science test. There's nothing wrong with that."

"Maybe, but you've got dark circles under your eyes and you've worn that same sweater every day for two weeks."

"It's cold out." Kylie pulled the worn sweater closer. "What does it matter what I look like, anyway?"

Okay, so she used to care a lot more about her appearance. And yes, she had been doing schoolwork around the clock. But was it really anyone's business?

Maybe you can relate. You go, go, go and then wonder why you're completely zapped. You were made for more than work. God wants you to rest in Him. No stress. Just complete and total relaxation.

There. Doesn't that feel good?

*Ah, I needed that, Lord! May I learn to lay
down my stresses and find rest in You. Amen.*

MORE THAN YOUR FEAR

*I sought the LORD, and he answered me
and delivered me from all my fears.*
PSALM 34:4 ESV

As a little girl, Elise would struggle to fall asleep because she was afraid of the ghosts under her bed. No one could convince her they weren't there. Her fears grew up alongside her as she aged. By the time she reached her teen years, she had irrational fears about diseases, strangers, and many other things as well.

When she finally made a really good friend—a true BFF—Elise got jealous when Aubrey had other friends besides her. She lashed out at her—fear triggering her insecurities—and one day her fears became a self-fulfilling prophecy. Aubrey gave up. She quit the friendship.

It took some counseling for Elise to come to grips with the fact that fear was quickly undoing her life. With the help of a Christian counselor, she came to understand the truth—there is no fear in love. God truly can—and will—cast out fear, if you let Him.

Maybe you're like Elise. Fear has ruled the day. It's time to kick it to the curb. You have nothing to fear. You were created for bigger things than that.

*Lord, I refuse to give in to fear. Thank You for
the reminder that I was made for more! Amen.*

MORE SOFTNESS OF HEART

That is why the Holy Spirit says, "Today when you hear his voice, don't harden your hearts as Israel did when they rebelled, when they tested me in the wilderness."
HEBREWS 3:7–8 NLT

God made you to have a soft heart. But what does that look like? Say you get into a big argument at school with a girl you used to be friends with. You say mean things. She says mean things. You walk away.

Weeks go by, but you never try to make things right. Instead, your heart gets really hard toward her. When you see her coming down the hallway at school, you walk on the other side. You turn bitter and cold.

This kind of situation is awkward, isn't it? God made that soft heart of yours to forgive others and mend fences. He longs for you to live at peace with as many people as you can. No, that doesn't mean you have to be friends with everyone. But keep that heart soft, girl!

Lord, I don't want to have a hard heart! I'm asking You to soften it. Show me how to forgive the ones I need to forgive so that my heart doesn't grow cold. Amen.

MORE TIME AWAY FROM ELECTRONIC DEVICES

No temptation has overtaken you that is not common to man. God is faithful, and he will not let you be tempted beyond your ability, but with the temptation he will also provide the way of escape, that you may be able to endure it.
1 Corinthians 10:13 esv

If someone asked you, "Hey, do you think you spend too much time on your phone or tablet?" what would you say? Or what if they asked, "How many hours a week do you spend playing video games, anyway?" Ouch!

Here's the truth: electronic devices can be very addicting. That's why you see so many people walking around with them in their hands all the time. But they should never take the place of time spent with real, live people. It's fun to text, sure. And video games can be a nice distraction. But God made you for so much more than that. He wants you to have face-to-face interactions with people and to do it with as much joy as you have when you text your BFF.

Give yourself a challenge. Put down the electronics for a few hours. Only allow yourself to check your social media account for messages from friends at a certain time of the day. Spend more time with God and with the people He's placed in your life. You'll be so glad you did!

Lord, I'm sorry about the hours I've wasted on electronics. Help me break any addiction, I pray. Amen!

MORE LOVING

*Above all, love each
other deeply, because love
covers over a multitude of sins.*
1 PETER 4:8 NIV

Some people say that love is a feeling, but here's the truth: love is a verb. It's an action. And it's not always easy to love people. (You've probably already figured that out.) When that younger brother of yours is mean to you all the time, it's difficult. Let's face it, living with an angry person is tough! When a friend hurts your feelings in front of others at school, the last thing you want to do is love them.

God commands us to love. He designed us to love. And He expects us to love, even when it feels impossible. Love doesn't mean you put your stamp of approval on negative behavior. It doesn't mean you extend mushy-gushy words to the one who's off course. It simply means that you exhibit the kind of love God would give you when you've fallen off the straight and narrow. You keep hoping, keep believing, keep trusting.

You were created to love, girl. Get to it!

*Father God, help me be
more loving, I pray. Amen.*

MORE TIME IN HIS WORD

*So then faith cometh by hearing,
and hearing by the word of God.*
ROMANS 10:17 KJV

Taylor loved to read. She devoured book after book—everything from novels to self-help books. You could most often find her curled up on the sofa (or in bed) with a book in hand.

When it came to reading her Bible, though, Taylor wasn't as excited. She skimmed verses here and there but didn't devour the Word in the same way she devoured the books she loved.

Why is that, do you think? Perhaps she didn't see it as a giant storybook, like a novel. Or maybe the "self-help" features weren't as easy to understand as a modern textbook.

The truth is, you were made to spend time in God's Word. God created you with a need, a desire, to know Him more, and part of the "knowing" comes by getting out your Bible and reading—not just a verse here or there, but whole sections at a time.

What are you waiting for, girl? Grab that Bible and dive in!

*Lord, I'm so grateful for Your Word. The Bible truly is
a lamp to my feet and a light to my path. Thank You
for sharing Your Word with humankind. Amen.*

MORE THAN YOUR PROBLEMS

*God is our refuge and strength,
always ready to help in times of trouble.*
Psalm 46:1 nlt

Problems, problems everywhere! Some days you feel like they'll never end. Your mom is mad at you. Your little sister is driving you crazy. Your science teacher is irritated that you forgot your homework. You have a headache that won't go away. . .and you have a major test coming up that you haven't had time to study for.

Here's the truth: there will always be problems. No matter your age, you'll still have to face them (and probably on a daily basis). It's how you handle them that matters. If you let them consume you (and take too much space in your thoughts), then they will become a stumbling block.

God made you for more than that! He wants you to see your problems through the filter of His love. He's big enough to handle them for you, but that means you have to let go of the overthinking and worrying. Give those problems to the Lord and watch Him take charge in a way you never could.

*Lord, I'm more than my problems. Today,
I place them in Your (very capable) hands. Amen.*

MORE PEACE, LESS ANGER

*Do not be quickly provoked in your spirit,
for anger resides in the lap of fools.*
ECCLESIASTES 7:9 NIV

You're mad. . .and you have a perfect right to be! Anyone would be, after what your (former) best friend said about you behind your back. Ugh!

Still, the tight feeling in your stomach and the pain in your shoulders from all the tension aren't making things any better. Maybe it would be best if you calmed down a little and took a few deep breaths. Your anger isn't fixing anything, after all.

We all go through seasons when our anger can get the best of us, but that's certainly not what God had in mind when He created you. He wants you to be at peace—in your heart, your attitude, and your thoughts. That's why He keeps whispering things like, *"Forgive her,"* in your ear. It's not easy, but it's for your benefit, not just hers. If you release this to God, then you won't have to carry the weight or the anger of it.

Embrace peace, sweet girl. It's so much better than being upset!

Lord, this isn't going to be easy, but today I give my anger to You. I'm having a hard time with it anyway, and I know You can handle it. Give me Your peace, I pray. Amen.

MORE THAN YOUR SHAME

*Instead of shame and dishonor, you will enjoy
a double share of honor. You will possess a
double portion of prosperity in your land,
and everlasting joy will be yours.*
Isaiah 61:7 nlt

Carrigan couldn't seem to let go of the shame of her past. It affected every decision she made and was a barrier to every friendship. If she could go back and change the bad things she had done, she would. But Carrigan would never have the opportunity to make right what she had wronged. One terrible decision with a so-called friend had resulted in guilt she couldn't seem to shake.

"You have to get past this, Carrigan," everyone said. "God has forgiven you. You need to forgive yourself." But every time she would think about releasing herself from the guilt, those old feelings would wash back over her once again.

God created us for more than our shame. The Lord doesn't want us to live in the past. And that cloak of shame is a garment from yesterday.

Forgive yourself. Whether you did it on purpose or not. No matter the consequences. No matter who or what or where or when. Forgive yourself. Allow God to wash you clean, once and for all.

*Lord, today is the day I let go of the
shame I've clung to, once and for all. Amen.*

MORE THAN YOUR SUFFERING

We can rejoice, too, when we run into problems and trials, for we know that they help us develop endurance. And endurance develops strength of character, and character strengthens our confident hope of salvation.
ROMANS 5:3–4 NLT

Isla went through many struggles in her young life. She battled cystic fibrosis and was hospitalized many times with lung issues. It seemed the suffering never ended, even as she got into her teen years. Sickness was her constant companion. Before long, she became identified as "Oh, Isla? The one with CF?" She hated that description but understood that people didn't mean to label her.

Maybe you've been labeled because of your suffering too. You're "Jessica, the one going through chemo," or "Mya, the girl in the wheelchair." You're tired of the labels but don't know how to get past them.

You were made for more than your suffering—either physical or emotional. No matter what label the world sticks on you, God calls you His precious daughter. So cast aside any name that doesn't fit and proclaim to the world, "I'm more than all that!"

You are, you know!

I am more than all that, Lord. And I'm so grateful You see me as such. Amen.

MORE SELF-CONTROL

But the Holy Spirit produces this kind of fruit in our lives: love, joy, peace, patience, kindness, goodness, faithfulness, gentleness, and self-control. There is no law against these things!
GALATIANS 5:22–23 NLT

You know you want it. You know you need it. Self-control. It's that thing that keeps you from eating cookie #3 or slice of pie #2. It's the extra "oomph" you need to refrain from making that sarcastic comment that's burning on the tip of your tongue. It's the little voice in your head that says, *Nope. Don't go there!*

You were made to show self-control, girl! That's why it's listed as one of the fruits of the Spirit. You can't do it on your own. No way. You need the Spirit of God to hold you back when you feel like going off on someone who has hurt your kid sister. You rely on Him to get you through when you're trying to stick to your homework assignment. Self-control is not your enemy; it's your friend, and the two of you were created to hold hands at every turn.

Jesus, I know You designed me to exhibit more self-control, but I'm going to need Your help. It doesn't come naturally to me, I'm afraid. Thanks for stepping in to help! Amen.

MORE BEAUTY AROUND YOU

In the beginning God created the heavens and the earth. Now the earth was formless and empty, darkness was over the surface of the deep, and the Spirit of God was hovering over the waters.
GENESIS 1:1–2 NIV

"Breathtaking!" You stare at the waters of the mighty Pacific, overcome by the sight of the waves striking the cliffs. They pound away with staggering force and then roll gently back out to sea.

"Amazing!" You marvel at the sight of the Rocky Mountains in the distance, capped in snowy white frosting. They take your breath away.

"Unbelievable!" You stared into the bright blue eyes of your newborn sister while listening to her make those adorable little coos and gurgles. Magnificent!

All of creation points to its unique Creator, who cared enough to make the skies a brilliant blue and to dress penguins in lovely tuxedos. He thought you needed to be pretty special too, so He designed you specifically, just as you are—part of this beautiful creation you're meant to enjoy.

Lord, thank You for creating such a colorful, breathtaking planet for me to live on. Every day is a feast for the eyes and heart. I'm so grateful. Amen.

MORE CONFIDENCE TO DRAW NEAR

Let us then with confidence draw near to the throne of grace, that we may receive mercy and find grace to help in time of need.
HEBREWS 4:16 ESV

Jasmine's family adopted a dog from a local shelter. He was the sweetest little thing—an eight-month-old retriever mix weighing in at twenty-nine pounds. She didn't know much about the pooch's background, but one thing was evident—he had clearly suffered some sort of abuse. This was clear every time she reached out to touch him. He would duck his head and lower his frame as if he was terrified.

It took several weeks of letting him know he was safe before the sweet dog finally came around. He ended up being her sidekick, the perfect, confident companion.

Maybe you've spent a few years ducking too. You haven't trusted God to treat you well. You think He'll be as cruel as some of the people you've known in your past. But God adores you. He's the perfect Master, one you can trust—totally, fully, and completely. So don't be afraid to draw near. He longs to spend time with you.

*Lord, today I choose to draw near to You.
I want to know You more. You are
a good, good Father. Amen.*

MORE POWER FROM THE HOLY SPIRIT

"But you will receive power when the Holy Spirit has come upon you, and you will be my witnesses in Jerusalem and in all Judea and Samaria, and to the end of the earth."
Acts 1:8 esv

Zoey felt like her batteries were only half-charged much of the time. It wasn't just the physical exhaustion; it was the emotional baggage she still carried from stuff that happened when she was a kid. There were days when she watched others—her friends, teachers, parents, and so on—move so easily through life. She wondered if she would ever reach that point herself.

The Zoeys of this world struggle with feelings of emptiness. They feel powerless and overwhelmed. Maybe you've felt that way at times too. You wondered if you had the energy to get out of bed in the morning, put on clothes, and go to school.

God made you for more than that, girl! He gives you the physical energy you need to keep going, but (even more important) He fills You with His Spirit so that you can do great things for His kingdom.

Not feeling it? Ask for an infilling today. Then. . .watch out! God is going to charge your batteries like never before!

Lord, today I ask for You to fill me up to the tippy-top with Your power! Amen.

MORE REJOICING

"The Lord your God is with you, the Mighty Warrior who saves. He will take great delight in you; in his love he will no longer rebuke you, but will rejoice over you with singing."
Zephaniah 3:17 niv

What does it mean to rejoice? Nevaeh wasn't so sure. Did it mean she had to go around with a fake smile plastered on her face all day in order to convince nonbelievers that Christians somehow had it better? She still faced difficult things in her life, and faking it didn't seem like the best way to go. People would see right through her if she faked it, anyway. She'd never been very good at acting. And she didn't believe God really wanted her to.

As she grew in her faith, Nevaeh began to understand that God's version of joy is a lot deeper than feelings. He wasn't asking her to fake a sense of joy but instead to trust in Him. He wanted her to see that He would carry her when she couldn't carry herself, that He would even perform miracles, usually when she least expected them.

God proved His delight in her in so many surprising ways that she finally found the joy she'd been looking for.

Lord, I'm so excited to see that You take delight in me! You rejoice over me with singing, Father. What a lovely image that is! Amen.

MORE CONFESSION

*People who conceal their sins will not prosper,
but if they confess and turn from them,
they will receive mercy.*
PROVERBS 28:13 NLT

You messed up. You didn't mean to, but you did. You told a little white lie, and before long it blew up like a sponge soaked in water. Your teensy-tiny lie grew into a massive one. You hoped no one would ever find out the truth, but now you've been caught. Your mom knows you've been lying. You wish you could take it all back, but it's too late.

Take a look at today's Bible verse. The Word of God says it won't go well for those who hide their sins. God made you for more confession. . .more opening up and talking about what you've done. It's not always easy, but it's so worth it!

Why is it better to get things out in the open? When you confess your sin, God is faithful to forgive. And things will go better with your parents if you're honest too.

No matter what you've been hiding, you can tell someone today. It will take courage to come clean, but you'll feel so much better when you do. No more secrets. Tell someone what you've done.

*I'm a little scared, but I'll confess
my sins, Jesus. Give me courage, I pray.*

MORE ANSWERS FROM ON HIGH

"He will call on me, and I will answer him; I will be with him in trouble, I will deliver him and honor him."
Psalm 91:15 niv

For hours, Peyton tried to reach her friend on the phone. She didn't answer. Peyton tried texting, but those went unanswered too. By the end of the day, Peyton was freaking out. Why would her friend avoid her this way?

The next afternoon, she received a text from her friend. Whew! She had dropped her phone in the kitchen sink and ruined it. Now she had a new one.

Maybe you've been there. You've lost your ability to communicate because your phone died. Or maybe you've been on the other end—you're the one making the calls that go unanswered.

Here's a fun truth: God will always answer when you call. His phone is never out of service. He's prompt too. You call. . .He answers. Just like that. And you can expect Him to continue doing that because the Word of God promises that when you call, He'll answer. He will respond because He adores you, girl.

I'm so glad You answer when I call, Jesus! You'll never leave me hanging. Amen.

MORE OPPORTUNITIES TO FORGIVE

*Be kind and compassionate to
one another, forgiving each other,
just as in Christ God forgave you.*
EPHESIANS 4:32 NIV

"You don't understand," Addison cried out. "She hurt my feelings. . .again. And this time I know it was on purpose. So don't expect me to forgive her. She'll just turn around and do it all over again, like she always does."

"You don't know that, Addy," her mother said. "Sometimes people hurt others without meaning to."

"I'm still not going to forgive her, and you can't make me!" Addison stormed off to her bedroom.

Maybe you can relate to Addison's problem. Forgiving someone who has hurt you in the past is really tough. There are some people you shouldn't go on being friends with. But you can break your ties to a person and still forgive them. In fact, you must forgive them, even the ones who've done the unforgivable. To hold them in unforgiveness is to hold yourself in prison. . .and that's no way to live, girl.

*Lord, You've given me ample opportunities
to forgive people for the pain they've caused me,
and today I choose to do just that. Show me how
I need to forgive even now, Father. Amen.*

MORE LIGHT IN THE DARKNESS

This is the message we heard from Jesus and now declare to you: God is light, and there is no darkness in him at all.
1 John 1:5 nlt

This world can get pretty dark at times. A lot of people don't even seem to believe in God anymore, let alone follow the Bible. If ever there was a time to shine your light, this is it, girl!

Oh, that idea scares you? Well, you're not alone. Some Christians get so nervous about speaking up that they stop shining His light. They're too worried about what their friends will think. Sad, right? People all around you are lost, and someone needs to light the way.

Jesus made you to shine bright. And it's not too late! You can begin to bring peace, hope, and joy to others by speaking positive words over their situations. When friends at school are going through tough times, you can be the one to offer to pray. This is how your light will shine in the darkness. It doesn't take much to bring a shimmer of hope. You can make a difference if you'll just let that light shine.

I needed this reminder to shine bright, Lord. Thanks for making me a lamp of encouragement to others. Amen.

MORE THAN YOU COULD ASK OR THINK

Now all glory to God, who is able, through his mighty power at work within us, to accomplish infinitely more than we might ask or think.
EPHESIANS 3:20 NLT

"I'd like to have a pink pony and a unicorn and some cotton candy!"

As a three-year-old, you wanted it all, didn't you? You wanted sunshine, lollipops, rainbows, great friends, princess parties, snow globes, trips to amusement parks, and every other wonderful thing your imagination could dream of.

You haven't changed much, truth be told. That anticipation of "more than you could ask or think" is straight from heaven. God has promised it to you in His Word. And the reason you feel comfortable asking for the impossible from God is because He is known for performing the impossible. Praying for a sick friend? He can handle it. Praying for your hard work to pay off so you get a fantastic grade on that big test? He's pretty good at granting requests like that too.

Of course, pink ponies and unicorns might be out of the question, at least for now, but don't be afraid to ask for just about anything else your heart desires.

I'm so glad You're a God who loves my requests, Lord! Thank You for providing so many of the things I've asked for over the years. My gratitude overflows! Amen.

MORE TRANSFORMATION

Do not conform to the pattern of this world, but be transformed by the renewing of your mind. Then you will be able to test and approve what God's will is—his good, pleasing and perfect will.
ROMANS 12:2 NIV

Change is hard. In fact, it's so hard that we most often resist it. But true and lasting change (what we would call transformation) is totally worth the effort.

Maybe you've already transformed. You've changed your thinking about something. You've shifted your attitude. And you see the world differently now that you've done that.

God designed you to appreciate and adapt to change. He created you for transformation. And He's not just interested in seeing your opinions about the basics: your favorite foods, for instance. He's in it for long and lasting change that morphs you into His image.

Yes, you were designed to transform into the image (or likeness) of God.

"How is that possible?" you ask. To be more like Him, you have to spend more time with Him. (It's a proven fact that we become more like the ones we hang out with, after all.)

Don't conform to the world. Be transformed into His image. Change your mind. Make it more like His.

I want to be more like You, Jesus! Help me in every area of my life, I pray. Amen.

MORE IN THE BATTLE

*You have armed me with strength
for the battle; you have subdued
my enemies under my feet.*
PSALM 18:39 NLT

Sometimes life feels like a never-ending battle. The skirmishes go on and on, even when you wish they would stop.

Here's the truth, girl: the war doesn't come to an end simply because you're tired or beaten down from the fighting. But God wants you to know that you are more in the battle. When you're facing enemies (invisible or visible), He will give you everything you need to overcome.

Where there has been a lack of courage, He will give courage, faith, stamina, and passion for those who are battling alongside you. And best of all, He has given you the equipment you need—His armor! Read Ephesians 6 to learn more about the full armor of God. It will keep you safe in the midst of the battle.

Here's the key: don't give up. Don't say, "I just can't." You can! With the Lord's hand in yours, you can. And you will.

*Lord, You built me for battle. I'm a she warrior,
moving along with Your strength, not my own.
(Have I admitted how glad I am it's not my own
strength that's required?) Thank You for the armor
and the power to keep going, Father. Amen.*

MORE PURPOSE FOR EACH DAY

God's purpose in all this was to use the church to display his wisdom in its rich variety to all the unseen rulers and authorities in the heavenly places. This was his eternal plan, which he carried out through Christ Jesus our Lord.
EPHESIANS 3:10–11 NLT

What if you woke up every morning and asked God, "Where are You taking me today?" and then fully expected Him to show you?

Wouldn't life change for the better if you really believed that the Creator of the universe truly had a plan and a purpose for each day of your life?

Maybe today you're supposed to let your best friend pour out her heart while you offer comfort and calm. Perhaps this is the day you're supposed to bake cookies for the older lady down the street. Maybe you'll discover this is the day you meet someone who's going to be a part of your life for years to come.

Trusting God with your moments is cool. . .and fun! Stepping out in faith also plays a role. But understanding that the Lord has a purpose—not just in the general sense, but every single day—that's the motivator!

*Lord, where are You taking me today?
I'm ready to go! Amen.*

MORE TRIUMPHS OVER YOUR ENEMIES

*The Lord is on my side as my helper;
I shall look in triumph on those who hate me.*
Psalm 118:7 esv

Tiffany couldn't figure out why that one girl at school named Madeline seemed to hate her. This girl would do anything and everything to make Tiffany look bad, especially in front of the teachers. She tried to fight back (or to catch Madeline in the act so she could prove what she was up to), but this chick was clever! She seemed to have a knack for making herself look good and others look bad.

Maybe you've been through something like this. An unexpected enemy rose up and did what he (or she) could to defeat you. You found yourself shocked, hurt, and confused.

God has a plan for your enemies! You were created to triumph over them. Does that mean every nasty person will automatically disappear from your life (or get caught in the act of hurting you)? Nope. Sometimes the story will twist and turn a bit. But in the end, in whatever way He chooses to handle it, God will cause you to triumph.

*Lord, I know You've got my back. I trust
You to guide me safely past any who
would seek to harm me. Amen.*

MORE FREEDOM FROM MOCKERS

Blessed is the one who does not walk in step with the wicked or stand in the way that sinners take or sit in the company of mockers.
Psalm 1:1 niv

God wants to deliver you from the hands of the mockers, girl. Those people who bite and snap and make fun of you are a pain, and God takes their negative actions very seriously. He wants to show you how to free yourself from them, while also showing His love to them in the process. (That's not easy, is it? Treating mockers with kindness? What?)

God also wants to rid *you* of any mocking you might be doing. (Let's be honest: we all have a sarcastic, mocking side.) Is there someone—or something—you've been making fun of? Someone you can't help but tease? If so, it's time to lay that down.

Mocking isn't part of God's plan. He created you for freedom—total and complete freedom in Him. That can come only as you rid yourself of the things that once held you bound. So turn your back on mocking once and for all.

Lord, it hurts to be mocked. And I'm sure I've hurt others with my sarcastic comments at times. Rid me of the desire to make fun of others, I pray. Amen.

MORE CONFESSION

If we confess our sins, he is faithful and just to forgive us our sins and to cleanse us from all unrighteousness.
1 John 1:9 esv

"I really don't want to talk about it." Brooklyn kicked the dirt with the toe of her shoe and stared at the ground.

"Why not?" her best friend asked.

"It's just too. . .hard." To talk about it would mean she had to come clean, to admit her fault. Why would she do that when she could hold it inside? Who was she hurting, anyway. . .besides herself? One day she would admit the truth, and when she did, God would fix things. She hoped.

Maybe you've been there. You're hanging on to a hidden sin, one you've kept buried beneath the surface. You know it will eventually come out, but for now it's just too hard.

God created you for more than that! He has designed you to live in freedom as you confess your sins and receive His forgiveness. But first you have to be honest about what you've done.

Is there anything you're keeping hidden today? It's time to open up and share—truly share—what has been covered in cobwebs.

Lord, I don't like peeling back the cobwebs to peer inside. The things I've done make me shudder. But You've forgiven me, and I'm so grateful for a second chance! Amen.

MORE TIME SUITED UP

*Put on the full armor of God,
so that you can take your stand
against the devil's schemes.*
EPHESIANS 6:11 NIV

Maybe you know that feeling—of being attacked by someone completely out of the blue. Later, as you describe the event, you use words like "I never saw that one coming!" or "I didn't even know she was mad at me! I was so shocked when she went off on me!" There's just no way to process it because it makes no sense to you.

Life is filled with battles, and many of them (illnesses, false accusations, broken friendships) come from out of the blue, just like that. They make no sense at all. That's why it's so important to be suited up in God's armor. He has a plan to protect you from the enemy, and you were created to be armed at all times.

So dress yourself each morning, girl! Put on the breastplate of righteousness, the shoes of peace, and so on. Then, when unexpected hits come—and they will—you'll be ready for them.

*Lord, I want to be suited up so that I'm completely
protected at all times. I don't know when the
enemy will strike, but he won't knock me down as
long as I'm suited up and ready for him! Amen.*

MORE BLANKETS OF LOVE

*Whoever would foster love covers over an offense,
but whoever repeats the matter separates close friends.*
PROVERBS 17:9 NIV

Love is like a big, cozy blanket. You can toss it over cold, nearly hopeless situations. . .and they warm up. It really is the answer to so many of the problems you'll face, especially those difficult relationships.

Is there someone in your life who needs a blanket of love? Perhaps this would be a good day to make a list of all those in need.

That elderly neighbor, for instance. The checker at the grocery store who always looks so sad. That postal worker who looks so troubled. Your dad, after a long day at the office. Your mom, when she's trying to figure out what to make for dinner. Maybe you could think of ways to brighten their day.

And while you're at it, why not think big? Why not send a note of encouragement to someone who has played a positive role in your life? He (or she) might need a boost today.

You were created to blanket people with love. Trust God to show you who, how, and when.

*Lord, there are so many people in my world who need
love. I want to play my part by encouraging them.
Show me who I can bless today, Father. Amen.*

MORE RIVERS OF DELIGHTS

They feast on the abundance of your house, and you give them drink from the river of your delights.
PSALM 36:8 ESV

If you've seen the movie *Willy Wonka*, you have some idea of what Loompaland looks like. It's a wonderland of edible delights—suckers, wrapped candies, chocolates, and so on—with a gooey chocolate river flowing through the center of it. (Sounds amazing, right?)

God's river of delights makes the Oompa Loompa river pale in comparison. One day you'll see it fully—when you spend eternity in heaven with Him. When that day comes, you'll see what you were destined for all along. . .more of every good thing.

Anything you could have dreamed of will be there. . . times ten thousand! All you could have longed for will be found inside the gates of heaven—streets of gold, gates of pearl, and mansions that will make any earthly homes look like cracker boxes! And all of it will be yours in abundance when that day comes.

Lord, I'm looking forward to heaven, not just to feast my eyes on the delights to come, but to see You face-to-face and experience Your glory in ways I can only imagine! How I praise You, Lord! Amen.

MORE THAN YOUR INSECURITY

*"Fear not, therefore; you are of more
value than many sparrows."*
MATTHEW 10:31 ESV

You can't stand to glance at your reflection in the mirror. You're so insecure about how you look! And when it comes to your schoolwork, you feel pretty insecure there too. Ugh. And when all those other girls start planning a party, you wonder if they'll even include you. You don't have much confidence that they want you to fit in.

Feeling insecure stinks, doesn't it? Lacking confidence can be discouraging. But God doesn't want you to feel that way. If you could grab hold of the truth—that your security is found in Him—you would never have to worry about insecurity again. You can place your full confidence, not in yourself, but in the One who created heaven and earth. If anyone can be trusted, He can!

Today, it's time to make a list of the areas of your life where you're feeling insecure. Maybe you'll list things like appearance, clothes, grades, relationships, or even money. Then go down the list and say the words, "I was made for more than _____" (fill in the blank with whatever you're struggling with).

There! Doesn't that feel good?

*Lord, I get it. My security is in You, not me!
Today I place my confidence, my trust,
and my hope in You. Amen.*

MORE SELF-DISCIPLINE

For the Spirit God gave us does not make us timid, but gives us power, love and self-discipline.
2 TIMOTHY 1:7 NIV

What does it mean to discipline yourself? Do you need a daily chart with "Do this; don't do that" written down? (Maybe! Some people do better with lists, after all.) Most girls really need to learn to say no to their wants. That last slice of chocolate cake? Give it to your kid brother. Those jeans you're dying to buy? Skip them! Those new shoes? C'mon now. Do you really need them?

Temptations are everywhere, but God made you to be disciplined. It's going to feel so good to be able to sponsor that child in a third-world country or help feed a family in need instead of buying something new for yourself. Honest. . .it is. God designed you to be generous, and that's not possible if you spend all your resources on things you don't really need. So here's a really good question you can ask yourself whenever you're facing any sort of temptation: "Do I *really* need that?" If the answer is no, then skip it, girl!

Thanks for reminding me that I can skip it if I don't really need it, Lord. I want to be more self-disciplined. Amen.

MORE STRENGTH FOR THOSE WHO HOPE IN HIM

*So be strong and courageous,
all you who put your hope in the Lord!*
Psalm 31:24 nlt

On a scale of one to ten, Paisley felt like her strength was in about the two range. Lately, she just felt zapped, as if every task that needed to get done was just too much. Making her bed before school? Sounded too exhausting. Doing her homework after school? Impossible.

Maybe Paisley's situation sounds extreme to you, but there really are people who struggle to the point of barely being able to get out of bed in the morning. Tasks seem overwhelming, so they simply don't get done.

God created you to have strength. Sure, there will be days when you're truly tired—when you've got a cold or stomach virus or other bug—but even then, He can provide supernatural strength so that your body can heal. Even if you're a "Paisley" (one who genuinely struggles on a daily basis), don't stop asking for God's healing and strength. What you cannot do on your own, He surely can do for you.

*Lord, I need Your strength. There are days
when I feel I can't manage. Then You sweep
in and supernaturally fill me. Thank You for
creating me to be strong in You! Amen.*

MORE PRAISE

Why, my soul, are you downcast? Why so disturbed within me? Put your hope in God, for I will yet praise him, my Savior and my God.
PSALM 42:11 NIV

You're going through a hard time. Everyone who knows you can see it. You couldn't hide it if you tried. Not that you feel like trying! After all you've been through, you've earned the right to cry. . .and so you do. The tears flow like rain.

And then a gentle whisper from the Holy Spirit reminds you that you were created for more than the pain you're feeling. You were designed to praise, even in the middle of the darkest situations. No, it doesn't make sense. But yet. . .it feels so right.

So you lift your head. You tilt your face toward heaven and cry out, "I don't get it, God, but I choose to praise You anyway!" Maybe others will think you've lost your mind, but you don't care. Praising your way through the storm is the way to go.

The pain doesn't go away, at least not completely. But over a period of time, as you praise your way through, tiny snatches of it slip away. And the power that comes from praise gives you strength to keep going, no matter how rocky the path ahead.

Lord, I praise You today. Things in my life aren't perfect. There are problems galore. But that won't stop my praise. I'll power my way through with Your help, Father! Amen.

MORE CONCERNS ABOUT ETERNITY

Yet God has made everything beautiful for its own time. He has planted eternity in the human heart, but even so, people cannot see the whole scope of God's work from beginning to end.
ECCLESIASTES 3:11 NLT

Forever.

Think about that word. What does *forever* mean to you? Sometimes you say things like, "Ugh, this is taking *for-ev-er!*" But is it really?

God wants you to have a different *forever* attitude about the problems you face in life. You were made to have an eternal perspective—one that thinks not just about this world, but about the world to come. Seeing your situation in light of eternity changes everything! Those heartaches you're facing right now? They'll be washed away in heaven. And that physical pain you're struggling with? There will be none of that.

When you're facing a tough situation and you're tempted to get upset, angry, or worried, ask yourself: "Is this an eternal problem or a noneternal problem?" If it's noneternal (most earthly problems are), then you need to shift your focus from here to eternity. Begin to develop a *forever* perspective even now.

Lord, thank You for the reminder that my problems won't last forever! I need an eternal perspective. Help me to see my situation the way You do, Father. Amen.

MORE ROOTS DEEPENED

I pray that out of his glorious riches he may strengthen you with power through his Spirit in your inner being, so that Christ may dwell in your hearts through faith. And I pray that you, being rooted and established in love, may have power. . .to grasp how wide and long and high and deep is the love of Christ.
EPHESIANS 3:16–18 NIV

The most beautiful oak tree shaded Aurora's front yard but, over time, caused massive problems. The tree's roots were shallow and bumpy. They messed up the grass and were a danger for the blades of the lawn mower, which her dad found out the hard way. Ouch! Before long, she couldn't even walk across the lawn without being careful not to trip or fall. If only the roots had traveled downward instead of outward. All their problems would have been solved.

There's a reason God wants our roots to go down deep. When we're not deeply rooted, any type of storm can come along and topple us. A broken friendship? Over we go. A fight with Mom? We tip and fall. A failing grade in school? It wrecks us!

You were made for deep roots, girl. Deeper and deeper still, as you age. Don't let the storms of life topple you. You're meant to stand. . .and stand strong.

Thanks for taking my roots down deep, Jesus. I want to stand firm! Amen.

MORE GOOD FROM BAD

We know that God makes all things work together for the good of those who love Him and are chosen to be a part of His plan.
ROMANS 8:28 NLV

"Don't get so worked up! Everything will turn out all right! What the enemy meant for evil, God will use for good."

If you were raised in church, you probably heard those words a lot. When your mom lost a job. When your friends deserted you. When illness hit hard and your grandmother was dying. There you were, in the middle of your struggle, and some well-meaning person had the nerve to say, "Look on the bright side! It's gonna be okay!"

When you're in the middle of a dark season, it's hard to look on the bright side. And sometimes cheerful words from a friend or loved one can feel more like a slap in the face. Don't they get it? You're hurting.

If you're ready to search the Bible for yourself, you'll find a ton of references to back up what your loved ones are *trying* to say. Their delivery might not be the best, but the truth remains—God really *does* want to bring good from the bad in your life. You were created for more victory stories. So don't get irritated. Take a deep breath. . . and open the Bible for the encouragement you need.

You designed me to find the good in the bad, Lord, and I'm doing my best! Amen.

MORE ESCAPES

The temptations in your life are no different from what others experience. And God is faithful. He will not allow the temptation to be more than you can stand. When you are tempted, he will show you a way out so that you can endure.
1 CORINTHIANS 10:13 NLT

Samantha lifted her pencil from the maze and studied it carefully. If she took this route right here. . .no, that wouldn't work. She ended up at a dead end once again. What about this route? She rested her pencil tip on the page and drew the line, but it too ended at a dead end.

Maybe you've been there. You've tried to figure out which way to go when you're in a hard situation but found yourself at dead end after dead end. No matter what you tried, you couldn't escape. After a while you felt trapped.

God never meant for you to feel trapped, girl! He made you to be an escape artist! Jesus is faithful. He won't let you be tempted beyond what you're able to endure. He always provides a way of escape—from that toxic friendship. From your fears. From feelings of hopelessness. From everything that has worried you since you were little bitty.

You weren't meant to carry the burden always. Eyes wide open! God is going to give you a way of escape!

Lord, my eyes are fixed on You. I don't want to miss the big escape! You're about to take me from pain to joy, Father, and I'm so grateful! Amen.

MORE THAN YOUR ENEMIES

"But to you who are listening I say: Love your enemies, do good to those who hate you, bless those who curse you, pray for those who mistreat you."
LUKE 6:27–28 NIV

Read nearly every great Bible story and you'll find a hero and an enemy. The mighty men and women of God always had people standing in their way. David had Goliath. Moses had Pharaoh. And the Israelites, of course, had a bunch of other nations that battled to take them down.

You've probably had a few enemies too. That girl who couldn't wait to spread lies about you. That teacher who—for whatever reason—enjoyed embarrassing you in front of the other students. That boy in fifth grade who always called you ugly or made fun of the way you dressed.

Life is filled with enemies, but remember, girl. . .you were made for more than that. Everyone has people who oppose them, so you're not alone. But even if you were, God would still be on your side. He wants you to know that He's got your back. He sees the injustices and the pain and will guard and protect you.

Do good to those who hate you. (Really?) Bless those who curse you. (Ouch!) Pray for those who mistreat you. That's God's recipe for the best possible payback.

Jesus, I'll do my best to see my enemies through Your eyes! Amen.

MORE GIVING

*Each of you should give what you have decided
in your heart to give, not reluctantly or under
compulsion, for God loves a cheerful giver.*
2 CORINTHIANS 9:7 NIV

When you hear stories about people going through a hard time, do they soften your heart and make you want to help them? Let's say you heard about a child in your neighborhood who had no shoes. You would want to do whatever you could to make sure he had at least one pair, maybe two. Right? Or if you found out that the elderly lady next door had no food, you would make sure she had meals, even if you had to cook them yourself.

You should definitely be moved by stories like these. God has given you His heart for these people, and you were made for more giving, more caring, more compassion. Keep your eyes and ears open to discover the needs of those around you, and then give as you feel prompted. Who knows? Maybe you'll lead by example and others will become givers too!

*Lord, I want to be a giver. Show me who, what,
when, where, why, and how, I pray. Amen.*

MORE OF HIS CALLING

*He. . .set me apart before I was born,
and. . .called me by his grace.*
GALATIANS 1:15 ESV

From the time Mirabelle was a little girl, she felt a call on her life to work with children. At church, she volunteered in the nursery. From there, she began to help out in children's church. By the time she reached her preteen years, Mirabelle was working nearly every Sunday.

Each week, as she took in those precious, sweet faces of the children seated in front of her, Mirabelle's heart soared. She laughed with them, taught lessons, put together puppet shows, even led worship. . .all out of a heart for the kids.

Maybe you've also felt a particular call on your life since you were little. Perhaps you feel led to raise money for missionaries or provide meals for families in need.

These "calls" are God breathed. They're not just good ideas you've drummed up. Doesn't it do your heart good to know that the Lord created and designed you to do significant things for Him? In fact, He has set you apart to do them, even before you were born. Wow! With a calling like that, how can you resist, girl?

*You've called me, Lord! Here I am,
ready to step out in faith! Amen.*

MORE POSSIBILITIES

"What do you mean, 'If I can'?" Jesus asked. "Anything is possible if a person believes."
MARK 9:23 NLT

Have you ever listened to someone tell a "what if" story? After you listened, maybe you shrugged and said, "I guess that's possible."

Life is filled with possibilities. There are many, many things that could happen. . .if we just believed. Lives could be turned around. Relationships could be restored. Finances could be fixed. Broken hearts could be mended. The possibility of all these things happening rises exponentially as your faith grows.

So what possibilities are you facing? Which ones are you saying, "Yes and amen!" to? Which ones have you given up on entirely? Have you secretly wondered if there's any chance at all at times?

It's time to trust God with the what-ifs. The possibilities are endless when you place the outcome of life's situations into His hands. They're mighty big hands, you know.

Lord, I'm opening my mind to the possibility that You can turn things around in any situation You choose. My eyes are wide open as I begin to expect miracles all around me. Amen.

MORE HELP FROM ON HIGH

Fear not, for I am with you; be not dismayed, for I am your God; I will strengthen you, I will help you, I will uphold you with my righteous right hand.
ISAIAH 41:10 ESV

"I need help." Reagan spoke the words, her voice quivering. Though she was terrified to let people know, she needed help and couldn't wait any longer.

She moved forward with the conversation, telling the officer about her situation with her boyfriend. He was abusive, and not just verbally. Things had crossed a line, and she needed to get out. But she needed help.

There truly are moments in life when you have to trust God to get you out of precarious situations—relationships that have gone awry, jobs that are threatening your emotional health, even friendships that have become lopsided. The Lord is okay with you exiting toxic relationships, and He's there to guide you to the people who can offer assistance.

Trust Him in the scary seasons. Keep your eyes wide open. More help is coming your way as long as you look to Him and trust His guidance.

Lord, I come to You—for the little things and the big ones too. Whom have I in heaven but You, my Helper, my Savior, my King? Amen.

MORE SUCCESSFUL PLANS

*May he give you the desire of your heart
and make all your plans succeed.*
PSALM 20:4 NIV

"God wants me to be a success?" Kennedy scratched her head as she pondered this notion. "How do you know?"

"Because," her friend replied, "He wants to give you the desires of your heart, and the Bible says He wants to make your plans succeed."

"Really?" Kennedy said. "Well, that changes everything!"

Wow, that's really something, isn't it? You were created to succeed. Think about that for a moment. The God of the universe wants you—little old you—to do great and mighty things for Him. You're His daughter, after all. Would you, as a parent, want anything less than success for your child?

So don't give up. Don't give in to feelings that you're a failure. You're not a failure. You were made for success, girl. Now dress for it—inside and out.

You have plans for my success, Jesus. I can't see them yet, but I know I can trust You. Today I give all my hopes, plans, and dreams to You. Amen.

MORE CONFIDENCE IN HIM, NOT YOU

Let us then approach God's throne of grace with confidence, so that we may receive mercy and find grace to help us in our time of need.
HEBREWS 4:16 NIV

"Square those shoulders! Stand up straight!"

Eliana replayed her mother's words in her mind time and time again. She couldn't seem to stop them.

"Act like you're confident even if you're not!"

Ack! She tried. Oh, she tried. But pretending to be confident required. . .well. . .confidence, and that was something Eliana didn't have.

Maybe someone says those things to you. You're struggling with your confidence. God wants you to know that He designed you to be confident, not in your own abilities but in His. You don't have to fake it. You don't have to pretend. (You probably do yourself more harm when you're acting.) Instead, seek the real deal. Real confidence is found only in Him not in yourself.

Confidence is found in You, Lord! I want the real deal not the cheater's version of confidence. No more faking it till I make it. I'll never make it without You, Father. Amen.

MORE REST FOR YOUR SOUL

*"Take my yoke upon you and learn from me,
for I am gentle and humble in heart,
and you will find rest for your souls."*
MATTHEW 11:29 NIV

We were only meant to carry certain weights. When we pick up burdens that aren't really ours to lug around, we're weighing ourselves down unnecessarily. Your friend's boyfriend problems? Sure, you need to care about her, but if you get in the middle of it, you'll have regrets. Your kid sister's squabbles with her best friend? Those aren't yours to fix. That fiasco going on between your BFF and her mom? Don't go there, girl!

The only way to find true rest for our souls is to carry the troubles that are meant for us, nothing more and nothing less. Pick up too much and you'll sink. Pick up too little and you won't learn how to handle problems as they crop up.

God designed your soul to be at rest. So, problems or no problems, you can rest easy in the fact that He's going to take care of you.

Jesus, I'm so glad my soul can rest in You. I'll admit, I've taken on some burdens that weren't mine to carry. They stressed me out! But You? You bring peace in the storm and rest when I'm wiped out. I'm so grateful. Amen.

MORE OF GOD'S PATIENCE TOWARD YOU

The Lord is not slow to fulfill his promise as some count slowness, but is patient toward you, not wishing that any should perish, but that all should reach repentance.
2 PETER 3:9 ESV

Patience. . .patience! It's not always easy to have patience.

But wait. Isn't that what God gives you, usually when you don't deserve it? If He's generous enough to pour it out for you, then you can do the same for others, right? He did design you to be more patient, girl. Don't believe it? Check out all the verses on patience in the Word of God. There are a ton of them!

Don't give up just because something isn't happening according to your timetable. Don't say things like "I guess God just didn't hear my prayer" or "I guess He doesn't care about the things that matter to me. He cares about others, just not me."

He does care. In fact, He cares enough to build a little character in you as you're waiting. So hang tight. You were made for more patience, girl. Start showing a little!

Lord, I'll try to hold on a little longer. I can't do it in my strength, but You can give me all I need to hold tight in the waiting. Amen.

MORE STRENGTH TO GET THE JOB DONE

*And let us not grow weary of
doing good, for in due season
we will reap, if we do not give up.*
GALATIANS 6:9 ESV

Kinsley was great at starting things. . .just not so great at finishing them. All you had to do was take a peek at the half-written essay to figure that out. Or the scrapbook she'd started. Or the before-school Bible study she joined but never attended. Starting was easy. Following through. . .not so much. She always seemed to lose interest and give up.

Maybe you can relate. You dive into a project with gusto but feel yourself zapped of energy a short while later. If so, there's great news for you today! God has created you for more strength to finish those tasks. It's true! You will reap a harvest in due season if you don't give up.

So don't quit. Get back up. Dust yourself off. Pray. Ask God to give you all you need. Then dive back into that half-done project. Get 'er done, girl. You were made to finish, and you'll be so glad you did.

*Lord, I want to be known as a woman who
finishes well. I don't want to quit halfway in.
Give me the strength and tenacity to finish the
tasks You place in front of me, Father. Amen.*

MORE GOOD DEEDS

*And let us consider how we may spur one
another on toward love and good deeds,
not giving up meeting together, as some are in
the habit of doing, but encouraging one another—
and all the more as you see the Day approaching.*
HEBREWS 10:24–25 NIV

Remember that line in *The Wizard of Oz* where the Tin Man is told he will be a "good deed doer"? Perhaps you've known a few of those people in your life. They care for the needy, pass out clothing and food to the homeless, provide scholarships for kids to go to college, take care of the sick and the elderly. In short, they're amazing, giving people who are others-focused.

God wants you to be a good deed doer. You were created to perform more and more good deeds. The longer you walk with Christ, the more natural these deeds should become.

We're meant to "spur one another on" (nudge each other) toward love and good deeds. Are you encouraging others to be a giver by giving yourself? Are you showing them how to care for the downtrodden by caring yourself?

There's more in you, girl. Give. . .and then give some more.

*Show me fun, creative ways to spread
joy to others with good deeds, Lord! Amen.*

MORE TIME FEELING PEACEFUL

*Let him turn away from evil and do good;
let him seek peace and pursue it.*
1 Peter 3:11 esv

Maya was always frustrated. On good days and bad, her frustration simmered like a kettle on the stove, just under the boiling point. Every now and again something—or someone—would cause it to boil over into anger. For the most part, though, she kept it under control as best she could.

Living with frustration can be hard. It's not something you wish for, is it, girl? In fact, most people wish they could get rid of it for good because it gets in the way of their relationships and zaps the joy from life.

How do you get rid of frustration? By spending more time asking God to fill you with His peace. When you grab hold of His peace, you let go of anything else that's threatening to hold you back. In many ways it's like taking hold of a life raft when you're in the river. You have to cling to it for dear life and never let it go.

*Lord, today I'm pursuing Your peace as never before.
I won't let the enemy rob me of it. It's mine for
the asking. Thank You, Father. Amen.*

MORE TIME IN GOD'S HOLY PLACE

He made the Most Holy Place 30 feet wide, corresponding to the width of the Temple, and 30 feet deep. He overlaid its interior with 23 tons of fine gold.
2 CHRONICLES 3:8 NLT

God made you to spend more time in His holy place. Are you wondering what that means? Do you have to search for a special temple or tabernacle where you can worship Him?

When you accept Jesus as Lord and Savior, He comes to live in a special tabernacle (dwelling place) in your heart. That's where He wants to meet you. It's not a physical building. He's right there, deep inside of you.

You can meet with Jesus and worship Him, bringing Him praise for all He's done in your life. Your quiet time with God is holy and precious. He longs to meet you there so that He can convince you that you are loved. (Isn't it cool to think about how much God loves you?) So what are you waiting for? Head to that secret place with Him today.

I want to meet with You in Your secret place in my heart. Thank You for loving me so much that You want to hang out with me, Father. Amen.

MORE STRENGTH TO START OVER

My flesh and my heart may fail, but God is the strength of my heart and my portion forever.
PSALM 73:26 NIV

Presley felt like giving up. She'd worked so hard on this project for her history class, only to have the computer swallow it whole at the last minute. All those hours of preparation. . .gone in an instant. She wasn't sure if she should cry or throw something at the wall. In that moment, piecing things together again—from scratch—seemed impossible. She didn't have the energy!

Presley pushed the laptop aside and tried to figure out what she would tell her teacher. He would be upset that she hadn't completed the assignment, but what could she do? After a moment, Presley released a slow breath. A glance at the clock showed her it was 7:30. If she worked really hard, really fast, she could probably redo the whole thing by ten o'clock then get some sleep.

And that's what she did. Her second go-round went more smoothly than the first, and the following morning she made a great presentation in front of her class.

Maybe you've been in similar situations. Something needs your immediate attention, and your heart just isn't in it. God wants you to know that He can give you the "oomph" you need to make it through, even when you're completely convinced you can't.

I need Your "oomph" today, Lord! Amen.

MORE REFLECTION

Now that which we see is as if we were looking in a broken mirror. But then we will see everything. Now I know only a part. But then I will know everything in a perfect way. That is how God knows me right now.
1 Corinthians 13:12 nlv

Pause. Reflect. Don't rush. Give it time.

There. That wasn't so hard, now was it?

We get in such a hurry that we rarely take the time to pause and reflect (think things through). But here's a fun truth: more of Jesus means more time thinking things through before acting. "Reflecting on what?" you ask. His goodness. His kindness toward you when you deserve otherwise. His great love for you—when you get it right and even when you get it wrong.

It's also good to reflect on the areas of your life that need change. When you really take the time to see the problem areas, you will be more likely to take the time to change them. (Changing isn't as scary as it sounds. . .promise!)

You were made for more "pause and think" time, girl. Never be ashamed to slow down and take the time you need to reflect on Him.

I need that time today, Jesus. I want to pause from my crazy life and reflect on You. Amen.

MORE PROTECTION

Though a thousand fall at your side, though ten thousand are dying around you, these evils will not touch you.
PSALM 91:7 NLT

Picture this: the battle is hot and heavy, and soldiers are dropping all around you. There you stand, watching them go down and wondering if you're going to survive. Your knees knock. You are overcome with fear. What do you do?

Fear is definitely not from the Lord. If you're facing a challenge—even the very biggest one of your life—you can still trust Him. God wants you to know that He's your Protector. That doesn't just mean He'll keep the enemy off your back. It means He's got you, even if you're facing a literal giant, like a life-threatening diagnosis or the loss of your home.

Being protected by God doesn't mean we won't go through challenges in this life, but it does mean that He's right there, walking through them with us. He's in the fire, the flood, the illness, and the pain. His protective hand guides, directs, and comforts. And He's working out a plan for your good.

You were created for more of His covering, more of His protection. Lean on Him today, no matter what you're going through. He won't let you down.

I will lean on You for protection, Jesus! When I let You be in charge, I don't have to be afraid. Amen.

MORE SMOOTHING THINGS OUT

*A friend loves at all times, and a
brother is born for a time of adversity.*
PROVERBS 17:17 NIV

Let's face it: hanging out with friends is fun...except when it isn't. Sometimes friends get into arguments over the silliest things. Maybe one wants to boss the others around or feels the need to be right all the time. What a pain! Or maybe one always gets her feelings hurt and ends up getting upset. It's so crazy, the things we allow to divide us.

Here's a great truth: God created you to smooth things out. He doesn't want those arguments to last forever. In fact, He'd prefer they not happen at all. But when they do, get over them quickly. Be ready to say, "I'm sorry." Be just as quick to say, "Apology accepted." Unruffle those feathers and step back in long enough to say, "Can't we all just get along?"

It doesn't matter who was right or wrong. That's often not the point. What matters is that you keep on forgiving and display the character of Christ by acting the way He would act. You were created for that, after all.

*Lord, thank You for the reminder that I can
(and should) smooth things out. I'll lay down
my pride and do the right thing, Father. Amen.*

MORE HOPE

*May the God of hope fill you with all joy
and peace in believing, so that by the power
of the Holy Spirit you may abound in hope.*
ROMANS 15:13 ESV

"Honey, you can't give up hope. You just can't."

Alexa leaned her head into her hands and cried. She hadn't stopped crying ever since she got the news that her best friend was moving away. How could her mom ask her not to give up hope now, with her best friend in the world moving to another state? Didn't she see how awful this was? How dare Mom try to fill her with hope at a time like this? She didn't want to be hopeful. She wanted to be sad!

Hope is more precious than gold or diamonds. It's more valuable than all the jewels in the royal crown. Hope is what keeps us going when everything around us screams, "Just give up, already!"

Hope is what we need when we don't know what we need. It's a propellant, a healer, an inspirer. Even more, it's something our heavenly Father wants us to have. We were made to be filled with hope, even in hopeless times. *Especially* in hopeless times.

*Jesus, You created me to have more hope,
even in times when it makes no sense.
I place my trust in You! Amen.*

More Comfort from the Father

*Even though I walk through the darkest valley,
I will fear no evil, for you are with me;
your rod and your staff, they comfort me.*
PSALM 23:4 NIV

When you're grieving—when the pain is so fresh you're doubled over from the sheer weight of the loss—you think you'll never smile again. Life will never be worth living. You'll never draw another breath without aching for the one you've lost. It seems impossible that the sun will continue to rise with breathtaking colors each morning and set again at night. How could it, when your world has been rocked so violently?

During this earth-shattering season, God's presence can be just as real as ever. In fact, He longs so deeply for you to be comforted that He draws close. Don't believe it? Read Psalm 23. You'll come to understand the words "Your rod and your staff, they comfort me" (Psalm 23:4 NIV).

God hasn't forgotten about you. He sees the pain. He knows the hurt. He's right there, arms extended, saying, *"Come to Me for comfort. I love you, My precious child, and I truly care."*

Sometimes the ache is so real that I wonder if I can go on, Jesus. During these seasons, I need You more than ever. Thank You for meeting me in my darkest valley. I'm not afraid as long as I know You're right there. Amen.

MORE POWERFUL PRAYERS

"Pray then like this: 'Our Father in heaven, hallowed be your name.' "
MATTHEW 6:9 ESV

Carly knew Mom had made a mistake, opening their front door to a salesman.

"This handy-dandy multipurpose cleaner will leave all your surfaces bright and shiny!" He held up a bottle of magic liquid and smiled. "Just spray it on your dirtiest spots, and you'll see instantaneous results!"

Carly doubted it, but her mom ended up buying a bottle just to get the man to go away.

Maybe you've tried miracle products before but were disappointed with the results.

Here's a fun fact: your prayers can be more effective than any magic potion or cleansing powder. They can do things you never dreamed they could do! Miracles can happen when you pray. And girl, you were made to believe that! God created you to believe that your prayers could move mountains.

So what's holding you back? Ready, set. . .pray!

I'm so grateful my prayers really work, Jesus. They're not like the products I've tried—all hype. You'll really work on my circumstances when I pray. I'm so grateful! Amen.

MORE CREATIVE IDEAS

*In the beginning God created
the heavens and the earth.*
GENESIS 1:1 NIV

Sadie was always coming up with awesome ideas for this or that. She was super-duper creative, and her art teacher loved her. She decorated her room in the cutest colors, and her clothes were fun and funky. Sadie seemed to overflow with creative ideas—things others didn't think of.

Maybe you're an ideas person too. That's good! You were created in the image of your very creative heavenly Father, after all, and He came up with quite a few clever ideas too. Like giraffes. And butterflies. And honeybees. (And to think, all of life got its start when God created the heavens and the earth!)

Don't be surprised when that next big idea comes. God might whisper it in your ear even now, if you listen closely enough.

*I'm so glad I was created in Your image,
God. I love my creativity. Use it for
Your glory, I pray. Amen.*

MORE FRUIT BEARING

"But blessed is the one who trusts in the Lord, whose confidence is in him. They will be like a tree planted by the water that sends out its roots by the stream. It does not fear when heat comes; its leaves are always green. It has no worries in a year of drought and never fails to bear fruit."
JEREMIAH 17:7–8 NIV

Gabby's family moved into a new house with a lemon tree in the backyard. She could hardly wait for summer so that she could pick lemons and use them for cooking, baking, and even drinking. (Homemade lemonade. . .yum!)

Unfortunately, the tree didn't produce any fruit that first year. Or the second. Gabby was sad! She checked out the internet for advice. There she learned that lemon trees take their time before bearing fruit.

Her parents began to take good care of the tree—pruning it, making sure it was fertilized and watered. Their work paid off when lemons burst through the third year.

Maybe you're like Gabby. You've planted seeds in a loved one—prayers, thoughtful deeds—and you don't see fruit yet. That person's behavior isn't changing at all! You're wondering if your "lemon tree" is ever going to bear fruit.

Don't give up, girl! You'll see fruit in God's perfect season! Don't stop praying, no matter what!

*Lord, I won't give up! I want to bear
fruit for Your kingdom. Amen.*

MORE ALERT

*Be alert and of sober mind. Your enemy
the devil prowls around like a roaring
lion looking for someone to devour.*
1 Peter 5:8 NIV

Amber was one of those girls who had a hard time falling asleep at night. Because of that, mornings were hard. She would wake up when the alarm went off, but not completely. A ten-minute snooze didn't do much to make her feel like getting up, but she had no choice. She had to go to school, after all. And though she was showered, dressed, and seated behind her desk an hour later, Amber still didn't feel fully awake. She couldn't seem to stop yawning!

Maybe you're like Amber. You're just not a morning person. And by the time you get to English class, you're still not fully there. It's one thing to live like that in the natural, another altogether to doze off in a spiritual sense. God designed you to be fully awake, girl! No falling asleep on the job for you! You have a very real enemy out there, and he would love nothing more than to take you down. So stay alert. Keep those eyes wide open. You have big tasks ahead of you, and they require you to be wide awake!

*I won't doze off and let the enemy
catch me off guard, Jesus! I'll be
alert and ready, fully engaged. Amen.*

MORE THAN YOUR HEARTACHE

*The Lord is close to the brokenhearted;
he rescues those whose spirits are crushed.*
Psalm 34:18 nlt

Hailey's father passed away unexpectedly. One morning he simply didn't wake up. He had died in his sleep. Hailey and her siblings were in a state of shock. So was their mother. How could God allow such a horrible thing to happen?

The next few weeks and months were a blur. She somehow made it through the funeral. But when the family had to move from the home they'd always lived in to an apartment, the pain hit all over again—this time a different sort of pain.

Maybe you've been through real heartache like Hailey's. Perhaps you've lost someone you love, or lost a pet, or been through the tragedy of a catastrophic storm.

Life will break your heart time and time again. But God doesn't want the pain to last forever. You are more than your heartache. He has good things planned for you on this side of the tragedy. Trust Him today—even if you haven't in days past. Put your hand back in His, and trust that He's going to take care of you from this day forward.

*Jesus, I trust You,
even in my pain. Amen.*

MORE OPPORTUNITIES TO BUILD OTHERS UP

*Therefore encourage one another
and build each other up,
just as in fact you are doing.*
1 Thessalonians 5:11 niv

Bella had a hard time bragging on others. She sang her own praises—a lot. But when it came to bragging on her friend who'd just snagged the choir solo or her younger brother who won the all-around trophy in baseball, she just couldn't seem to get the words to come out.

It wasn't that she wasn't happy for them, exactly. But when cool things happened to others, sometimes she felt like she was a loser. And she hated that feeling.

Maybe you can relate. You're happy when good things happen to those you love. Mostly. But sometimes all the applause they get makes you feel "less than."

God created you to sing the praises of your loved ones, to make a big splash when they've done something awesome. You were designed to encourage more, love more, and build each other up in good times and bad. Taking your eyes off yourself is step one. Step two. . .start encouraging others, girl!

*Jesus, help me take my eyes off
myself so that I can sing the
praises of others today. Amen.*

MORE JOY

The Lord is my strength and shield. I trust him with all my heart. He helps me, and my heart is filled with joy. I burst out in songs of thanksgiving.
Psalm 28:7 nlt

As a child, you probably sang about it. You had the "joy, joy, joy, joy down in your heart!" And you did! No doubt, childish giggles followed the singing of the song. You simply couldn't help yourself.

These days, the joy isn't always as easy to find (or to sing about). Your best friend isn't speaking to you. You got a C on your science test. Your dog has fleas. And there you are, in the middle of it all, trying to act like everything's perfect when it's not. (Not much joy in that, is there?)

Well, maybe there is! God created you for more joy! More in the bad times, more in the good. More in the chaos, more in the pain. More in the upswing, and more in the down.

Joy is an energy booster. It's like taking a great vitamin! Joy is God's gift to you—a bubbling, untroubling present that lifts your spirits on unliftable days.

He designed you to have the joy, joy, joy, girl. So let it flow!

*Jesus, I'm here, arms uplifted,
ready to receive Your joy! Amen.*

MORE UNDERSTANDING

*Whoever is patient has great understanding,
but one who is quick-tempered displays folly.*
Proverbs 14:29 niv

Maybe you've heard the expression "Try to see it from my point of view." People always say that when they think you're being unreasonable or self-focused, don't they? It's not easy to change your perspective, but when you shift your point of view, when you really try to see the situation through the eyes of the other person, you have to admit. . .things look different.

So what situations are you going through today? Do you need a different point of view? Have you been too "me" focused? Is it time to give someone else a turn?

God wants you to love others the way you love yourself. You were made to think of them not just yourself. So offer more understanding to those you love. Give them the benefit of a thoughtful response when they speak to you, even if you're not a fan of their tone of voice. God will honor your understanding.

*Lord, You've made me to be more understanding.
Obviously, I'm going to need help with this one!
Help me when I need reminding, I pray. Amen.*

MORE POWER FROM THE SPIRIT

May the God of hope fill you with all joy and peace as you trust in him, so that you may overflow with hope by the power of the Holy Spirit.
ROMANS 15:13 NIV

Piper felt like a spiritual wimp much of the time. Whenever the enemy would show up, she would cower in the corner. No fighting. No authority. Just. . .defeat, often before the battle even got under way.

God never intended our spiritual journey to be one of defeat. We were made for more power from the Holy Spirit. We've been given authority in the name of Jesus to combat the evils of this world, so we can't sit by while the enemy steals, kills, and destroys. We have to take a warrior's stance. . .with no apologies!

Are you feeling the power of the Spirit today? If not, ask for a fresh filling. The more you ask the Spirit of God to fill you, the stronger you'll be. And girl, you were created to be very strong in Him!

*I'm stronger than I know, Jesus!
Through the power of Your Spirit, I can
do great and mighty things for You. Amen.*

MORE GLORY

*For I consider that the sufferings of this
present time are not worth comparing
with the glory that is to be revealed to us.*
ROMANS 8:18 ESV

Have you ever looked at something through a filter? Maybe you've applied a filter to a photo you took. It changed everything. Gone were the pimples, the double chin, the freckles. The filter took care of all of that. Now you look like a supermodel!

There's a filter that God wants you to see all of life through, and that's His glory filter. His glory has been revealed to us, and it changes (literally) everything. The pain of a loved one's death? Changed when you glimpse it through the glory veil. The agony of losing a loved one? Eased, when viewed through His glory.

The way we see things changes when we look through the lens of eternity! Suddenly, the troubles of this life are teensy tiny in comparison to the joy that is to come.

You were created for more glory, girl! Put that filter in place, and see how the world changes!

*My sufferings cannot compare to the
glory of Your presence, Jesus. Thank You
for giving me an eternal perspective. Amen.*

MORE SACRIFICE

And so, dear brothers and sisters, I plead with you to give your bodies to God because of all he has done for you. Let them be a living and holy sacrifice—the kind he will find acceptable. This is truly the way to worship him.
ROMANS 12:1 NLT

Sacrifice sounds like a dirty word, doesn't it? To sacrifice something means you have to give it away. But what if you don't want to? Life gives us plenty of opportunities to give up things we don't *want* to give up, after all.

But God's views on sacrifice are far different. He views our sacrifices as a gift. That time you spent baking cookies for the elderly neighbor? A lovely sacrifice. The money you gave up so that your loved one could have what they needed? A beautiful gift.

You were designed to sacrifice—everything from your selfish desires to your body—and all in service to the Lord. He's not stealing anything from you. On the contrary, He offers lovely opportunities to give, because giving (sacrificing) grows you into a precious, selfless young woman.

Jesus, I can't believe I'm saying this, but I want to sacrifice more! When the ideas are Yours, not mine, You make provision. You have a lovely and perfect plan. So show me how and where to give, I pray. Amen.

MORE ABUNDANCE

Now to him who is able to do immeasurably more than all we ask or imagine, according to his power that is at work within us, to him be glory in the church and in Christ Jesus throughout all generations, for ever and ever! Amen.
Ephesians 3:20–21 niv

Most of Serenity's siblings and cousins had no trouble coming up with a Christmas wish list. They wrote down dozens of items—everything from the latest, greatest electronic gadgets to their favorite dolls and toys.

Not Serenity, though. She couldn't seem to make herself "wish" for anything. It seemed almost selfish. So she thought about it until she finally managed to write down one or two ideas for things that weren't terribly expensive. Her mom was startled and asked her to rethink the list.

Sometimes we approach God like Serenity approached her Christmas list. We're afraid to ask Him for the big stuff, so we shrug and say, "Whatever You think, God. Don't put Yourself out."

Oh, but He wants to put Himself out for you! One of the Lord's greatest desires is to lavish His children with unexpected treasures and joys. So don't be surprised when He goes exceedingly, abundantly above all you could ask or think. That's the kind of God He is!

I'm so grateful I can come to You with everything, Jesus! Those wishes and dreams are nothing compared to the things You've cooked up for me! I can't wait to see what You've got up Your sleeve! Amen.

MORE ATTITUDE CHECKS

For the word of God is alive and active. Sharper than any double-edged sword, it penetrates even to dividing soul and spirit, joints and marrow; it judges the thoughts and attitudes of the heart.
HEBREWS 4:12 NIV

Kaylee could be a little on the. . .well. . .snippy side. She didn't mean to be, but her rude behavior often upset others. More than once when she was a child, her mother would say, "Check your attitude, Kaylee!" Only one problem: she didn't know how. She would try, but then her temper would flare all over again.

Over the years, God showed Kaylee how to keep her temper in check and how to treat others kindly, even when she didn't feel like it. All she had to do was imagine how Jesus would respond to each person. Once she caught a glimpse of that, the rest was easy.

What about you? Do others in your world have to mutter the words "Attitude check!" whenever you come around? If so, it's time to see people through the eyes of Jesus. No one in the history of. . .well, ever. . .had to ask Jesus to check His attitude!

*I don't want to have to check my attitude.
I want Your mind and attitude, Jesus!
Help me with that, I pray. Amen.*

MORE PROMISES FULFILLED

"When you pass through the waters, I will be with you; and when you pass through the rivers, they will not sweep over you. When you walk through the fire, you will not be burned; the flames will not set you ablaze."
Isaiah 43:2 niv

Have you been through rough seasons in your life? Have you gone through waters so deep you thought you might drown? Have you faced fiery trials so fierce you felt you might be consumed?

Life is filled with challenges, but think about this: sometimes we see the hand of God at work even better when we're going through tough stuff. In the deep waters, He promises, *"You will not drown."* When the flames lap at you, the heat in your face more than you can stand, still He whispers, *"You will not be burned."*

God's promises are going to be fulfilled in your life no matter how deep the valleys get. When He says it. . .He means it. You were created to see His promises come to pass, so hold on tight! He has big things planned for you, girl, and no tough season is going to stop that!

Jesus, sometimes I think I've gotten so used to disappointments that I stop expecting Your promises to come to pass. People have let me down, but You never will. What wonderful news, Father! Amen.

MORE OPPORTUNITY FOR WISDOM

Be very careful, then, how you live—not as unwise but as wise, making the most of every opportunity, because the days are evil.
EPHESIANS 5:15–16 NIV

Did you realize that wisdom is something you have to choose? Several times a day you'll be presented with opportunities to decide: Do I choose wisely or foolishly?

God designed you for more wisdom, girl! He doesn't want His reputation to be ruined because you—His representative here on earth—lived in a way that dishonored Him or made Him look bad to others. When you live as one who is wise, you bring honor to Him and to yourself.

Be careful how you live. Make the most of every opportunity. Why? Because the world is watching. People are looking to you to lead by example. You say you're a Christian. . .they want to see if you're going to act like it.

Are you acting like it? Are you operating in godly wisdom? That's exactly what the world needs to see.

Jesus, I want to honor You by choosing wisdom in every situation. I know others are watching. Help me to make the right choices, I pray. Amen.

MORE CHAINS BROKEN

About midnight Paul and Silas were praying and singing hymns to God, and the other prisoners were listening to them.
Acts 16:25 NIV

Carolina was done with overeating. She was going to start watching what she ate. Only, the next time temptation hit, she found herself giving in. . .again. Afterward, she always felt awful, riddled with guilt and remorse.

Maybe you've battled addictions too. You feel chained to gossip. Or sugar. Or lying. You can't seem to stop, no matter how hard you try. The vices are real, and they keep you bound up until you can't breathe.

Chains are deadly at times. They fasten around you and refuse to let go. You're like a pup chained to a spike in the yard, the chain getting all twisted up as you fight to free yourself.

God longs for you to be set free—not just from the obvious addictions, but from other ones as well. Bitterness. Hatred. Jealousy. These are all chains that can keep you in bondage.

You weren't created for chains. You were made for more than that. God created you to be set free in Him—from all the things that seek to bind you.

Jesus, I'm done with these chains! I want to be set free permanently! Give me Your willpower. Break every chain, I pray! Amen.

MORE DESIRES OF YOUR HEART

Be happy in the Lord. And He will
give you the desires of your heart.
PSALM 37:4 NLV

If someone were to ask, "What are your deepest, fondest desires in life?" how would you answer? Most of us don't think we'll actually get the things we desire, so we're afraid to voice them aloud. Or maybe we're worried we *will* get what we desire, and we won't be able to handle it!

You were created to receive the things you desire, but it's clear (based on this scripture) that the key is found in delighting in the Lord. When you're in relationship with Him, when you place your love for Him above all else, then your desires line up with what He wants for your life. In other words, they're safe, healthy, God-breathed desires.

Don't be afraid to ask the Lord for the things that you feel called to have—friends, a good education, and so on. He just might surprise you with the ways He fulfills those desires, so watch out! God has an amazing imagination, after all.

I trust You with my desires, Lord. You know best,
so I ask You to fulfill my hopes, wishes, and dreams
in ways that only You can, Father! Amen.

MORE HUMILITY

*Do nothing out of selfish ambition
or vain conceit. Rather, in humility
value others above yourselves.*
PHILIPPIANS 2:3 NIV

What a me-me-me world we live in. Billboards, magazine ads, TV commercials, and infomercials all scream the praises of me, myself, and I. We're supposed to take care of ourselves—our hair, clothing, skin, and makeup—above all. It's all about us, if these ads are to be believed.

Only, it's not all about us. If you read the Bible carefully, you'll notice that it was never meant to be. Does that mean it's wrong to take care of your skin, hair, and so on? Of course not. God wants you to honor the vessel He's given you. But He's not keen on you spending all day hyperfocusing on that stuff. Is it critical to have the newest, most expensive electronics or a fancy house you can brag about? Not really. Why? Because you were designed to be humble, to do nothing out of selfish ambition or vain conceit. You were called by God to value others above yourself. It's not always easy—especially when it comes to the "stuff" you want—but it's always right.

*Lord, I have nothing to prove—to my neighbors,
my friends, or even myself. I humble myself
today and ask that Your will be done. Amen.*

MORE GLIMPSES OF HEAVEN

*"He will wipe away every tear from their eyes,
and death shall be no more, neither shall there
be mourning, nor crying, nor pain anymore,
for the former things have passed away."*
REVELATION 21:4 ESV

Maybe you've read stories about people who died, had a sneak peek of heaven, and then returned to their bodies here on earth. It's remarkable to think that these tiny glimpses into the vast unknown have had so many similarities.

Heaven is going to be a remarkable place. If you used your imagination to guess what it would be like, you'd only scratch the surface.

No more pain. No more tears. Spending eternity in worship to the One who makes all things new. Streets of gold. Rivers surrounding the throne of God. Wowza! It's going to be amazing!

There's only one way to get a true picture of heaven, and that's to assure yourself you're actually going there someday. You can settle that question today by accepting Jesus as Lord and Savior and asking Him to live in your heart. Once that's done, you're on your way to a blissful eternity!

*Jesus, I was created to spend eternity with You!
I can't wait for that day. Thank You for giving
me tiny glimpses even now. Amen.*

MORE ATTENTION TO YOUR WORDS

"For it is by your words that you will not be guilty and it is by your words that you will be guilty."
MATTHEW 12:37 NLV

You didn't mean to say it. The thoughtless words just slipped right out of your mouth. (Oops!) You criticized someone you care about and ended up hurting her feelings. Now she's upset, and you don't blame her! You wish you could take it back. If only you had never said something so mean in the first place. Why, oh why did you mess up like that, and how can you fix it? Will she ever speak to you again? (You wouldn't blame her if she didn't!)

The truth is, words matter. . .and God made you to speak lovely ones not ugly ones. He wants you to pay attention to the things that come out of your mouth.

Jesus said, "For it is by your words that you will not be guilty and it is by your words that you will be guilty." It's obvious the Lord takes your words very seriously. He says that they will make you either guilty or not guilty. Ouch! If Jesus takes your words seriously, it's time you did too. Don't carelessly throw them around. Pray and ask God to show you how to bless others with your words.

Lord, I want to bless others with my words. Help me, I pray. Amen.

MORE THAN BROKEN

"I have told you all this so that you may have peace in me. Here on earth you will have many trials and sorrows. But take heart, because I have overcome the world."
JOHN 16:33 NLT

"Oh no!" Hannah let out a scream as the beautiful vase hit the floor. Water covered everything in sight, and her mother's gorgeous roses—a surprise gift from Dad—went tumbling out onto the floor. Her mom came rushing her way. Instead of chewing her out, she knelt down on the floor and helped her clean up the mess.

You can glue a broken vase back together again, but what do you do with a broken life? Maybe you've been like that vase—tragically shattered into a thousand pieces. You didn't cause the situation. You had no control over it. But the pieces lay scattered all over the floor.

Only God can put together what has been broken in your life. Do you trust Him to do so? Today is a terrific day to acknowledge that you were made for more than brokenness. Let Him mend you so that you may be whole.

Jesus, I give You every broken piece. Do the kind of mending that only You can. Amen.

MORE CHANCES TO START OVER

If we confess our sins, he is faithful and just to forgive us our sins and to cleanse us from all unrighteousness.
1 JOHN 1:9 ESV

You blew it. Like. . .you really, really blew it. And time travel is sounding really good right about now. You're wishing you had a chance to go backward in time by a few hours and do things differently. But you can't. Life doesn't work like that. You have no choice but to move forward from here, hard as that might be. And somehow, you need to fix what you messed up.

God sees your heart, girl! Take that weight to Him. Ask for forgiveness for the thing you did wrong, but then learn to forgive yourself. In a way, His forgiveness really does give you a chance to start over. Of course, you'll still have to make things right with the people you hurt, but you're going to be able to do that with God's help. He's the King of second chances and will give you exactly the right words to say.

I'm so glad my mess-ups don't have to stop me in my tracks, Jesus. You can help me fix things. You are so good at second chances. I need one today! Amen.

MORE PEACEFUL REQUESTS

*Don't worry about anything; instead,
pray about everything. Tell God what you
need, and thank him for all he has done.*
PHILIPPIANS 4:6 NLT

"Just calm down, Gina. I can't understand what you're saying." McKenna leaned down and wiped her kid sister's eyes.

The four-year-old gulped in air and then hollered, "I. . .I. . .I fell down and hurt my knee!"

McKenna checked out her sister's knee and, sure enough, found a scrape and a bruise, which she bandaged.

Sometimes we're like that four-year-old. We come to God so worked up, so filled with emotion, that we blurt out nonsensical things to Him. In those moments, we can't see past the emotion of pain to string words together into a sensible sentence.

You were designed to offer peaceful requests to the Lord, even in seasons of chaos. So take a deep breath, girl. Gather your thoughts. Then make your requests known to God. He's right there, ready to meet you at your point of need.

*Jesus, I'm calm. Finally! I've taken a deep breath.
Now I'm ready to come to You, emotions aside,
to make my requests known. Thanks for giving
me peace in the chaos. Amen.*

MORE THAN YOUR PAST

Listen to me, O royal daughter; take to heart what I say. Forget your people and your family far away.
Psalm 45:10 nlt

Some people wear their past mistakes like their favorite T-shirt. They put it on before walking out the door in spite of the fact that it no longer fits. Maybe weeks, months, or years have gone by, but they're still stuck in that shirt, as if God hadn't forgiven them.

You're not a product, victim, or shameful example of your past. It does not define you. It doesn't hold a sign over your head saying, "Listen, everyone! This girl right here used to be a total loser! What a fiasco! She messed up everything! Just ask me and I'll tell you!"

Aren't you glad your past isn't making such a terrible announcement about who you used to be? You're not that girl anymore. You were made for more than your past. It's over. Done with. Never to be thrown in your face again. God has forgiven you and set you free. The garment of freedom is the only one you need to wear. Hallelujah! You were made for more.

Jesus, I'm so glad You've forgiven me for the sins of yesterday. Thank You for an amazing today and a hopeful tomorrow. Amen.

MORE EMOTIONAL HEALING

In his kindness God called you to share in his eternal glory by means of Christ Jesus. So after you have suffered a little while, he will restore, support, and strengthen you, and he will place you on a firm foundation.
1 Peter 5:10 NLT

Your emotions have been wrecked. Between the best friend who lied about you and the problems going on at home, you're about to lose it. And you're not sure you'll be able to get it together again if you do.

Today, there's good news for you! God never intended for your emotional suffering to last a lifetime. All along, He has had a plan for the healing of your heart and mind. In His kindness, this verse says, He called you to share in His glory. That kindness brings what you need the most: restoration, support for your soul, strength as only He can give. And, ultimately, a firm foundation to walk on after the crisis has passed.

You were created for emotional healing, not a lifetime of endless pain. Begin to lift your heart and your eyes, even now. No matter how deep the waters, no matter how badly you've been hurt, God is right there, offering a hand of kindness. Even now, He longs to make you whole.

I feel like I've been through so much pain in my life. Sometimes it seems unfair when I compare my journey to others'. But You, Jesus, have healed me when I needed it most. Thank You! Amen.

MORE GENEROSITY

"But who am I, and who are my people, that we should be able to give as generously as this? Everything comes from you, and we have given you only what comes from your hand."
1 CHRONICLES 29:14 NIV

You feel that little nudge in your heart whenever you notice a homeless man on the corner. Your heart aches when you watch infomercials about children in cancer hospitals and little ones starving in third-world countries. In other words, you care. . .and that's a good thing.

God created you to be more generous. Don't you love that? If you're a giver—and you're His child, so you surely are—then you already know it's more blessed to give than to receive. But what if you had more. . .so that you could give more? What if you were able to stock an elderly neighbor's pantry or cover the cost of a doctor visit for a friend with no insurance? What if you could sponsor a teen on a mission trip or support a child in a developing country?

He wants to bless you, not so that you can have the finest clothes, shoes, and so on, but so that you can be a blessing to others. It feels so good to help, doesn't it? And you'll be able to, as long as you keep the right perspective. Say the words, "I'm blessed to be a blessing!" and mean them.

You made me for generosity, Jesus. I'm not supposed to be stingy with my time, talents, or treasures. I'll give them freely for You. Amen.

MORE WALKING BY FAITH

*For we walk by faith,
not by sight.*
2 CORINTHIANS 5:7 ESV

Poor Hansel and Gretel. They dropped crumbs all along the path, hoping to find their way back home again. Unfortunately, the crumbs were eaten by birds, and they were lost in the woods indefinitely.

When you lose your way—when the crumbs aren't evident—how do you respond? Do you panic? Do you sit underneath a shade tree and give up? Do you feel like there's no hope that things will ever turn around?

God wants you to trust Him, even when you're feeling lost, even when there's not a scrap of bread to guide you anywhere. He wants you to look to Him—and Him alone—so that He can guide you exactly where you need to go. No fear. No questions. Just faith in the One who knows your path better than you ever could.

You were designed by God to walk by faith, girl. What's stopping you?

*Lord, I will walk by faith. I'll let go of
the reins of my life and trust You with
the details, even when I'm not sure where
You're taking me. I trust You, Lord. Amen.*

MORE LIKE JESUS IN YOUR BEHAVIOR

*A man of many companions may come to ruin,
but there is a friend who sticks closer than a brother.*
PROVERBS 18:24 ESV

"Monkey see, monkey do."

You've probably heard that expression at some point in your life. No matter which monkeys you hang out with (get it. . .hang out with?), you're liable to start acting like them.

Little children excel at it. They learn to walk, talk, and play by mimicking others, after all. And it doesn't stop there! This copycat behavior is especially evident during the teen years when kids swap attitudes and habits with one another.

Look, you know how this goes: if you hang out with girls who gossip, you'll probably start gossiping. If you hang out with teens who are determined to grow their relationship with the Lord, you'll probably end up stronger in Him too.

It's time for a monkey-check. Look around your cage and see who's close by. Are they pulling you away from God or pushing you toward Him? You might want to edge away from the monkeys who are setting a bad example.

*I want to be more like You in the way I act, Jesus.
I don't want to give You a bad name. I'll do my
best to pull away from the ones who might
deliberately cause me to stumble. Amen.*

MORE PLEASURE IN HARD WORK

Anything I wanted, I would take. I denied myself no pleasure. I even found great pleasure in hard work, a reward for all my labors.
ECCLESIASTES 2:10 NLT

Would the people who know you best say that you're a hard worker? Do you do your tasks with energy and joy? God loves a hard worker. In fact, He created you to be one!

Sure, sometimes you wonder if the things you're doing are making a difference. You work, work, work on a school paper, but who's going to remember it fifty years from now? You slave away organizing your room, but it just gets messy again.

Here's the truth: your work does matter! It matters to God, of course. It matters to your parents. They're watching closely to make sure you do the things you say you'll do. It matters to your teachers and to your friends. Whether you realize it or not, they're watching the things you do. Most of all, though, it matters to you. The person who gets the most out of your hard work is you!

Sure, it's tough to keep going sometimes. You get tired. But remember, Jesus never gave up. He worked hard to pay for your salvation.

I won't give up, Jesus! I'll work harder than ever. . .with Your help. Amen.

MORE LESSONS FROM THE HOLY SPIRIT

"But when the Father sends the Advocate as my representative—that is, the Holy Spirit— he will teach you everything and will remind you of everything I have told you."
John 14:26 NLT

Remember when you were a little kid, how you wanted to color a picture but couldn't seem to stay inside the lines? Your teacher told you to keep working at it, and you finally got it right. Now your coloring skills are stellar!

That's how it is with the Holy Spirit. He's a gentle teacher, giving you all the time you need to grow and develop into the person you'll one day be. He's your Helper, your Guide, your Friend. And you were made for more time in class with Him.

Not sure what that looks like? When you're praying, say, "Holy Spirit, come and lead me. Guide me. Teach me what I need to know so that I can be all You want me to be. Fill me every day so that I overflow!"

When you get serious with the Lord, He grows you into a person of great strength. And it's by His Spirit that you learn all the lessons you'll need to get there.

Lord, I'm so excited about what You're doing in my heart. I am a student! Holy Spirit, You are my teacher. May I learn every lesson so that I can be more like You, I pray. Amen.

MORE KINDHEARTED

Put out of your life all these things: bad feelings about other people, anger, temper, loud talk, bad talk which hurts other people, and bad feelings which hurt other people. You must be kind to each other. Think of the other person. Forgive other people just as God forgave you because of Christ's death on the cross.
EPHESIANS 4:31–32 NLV

Have you ever felt your heart growing harder and wondered what you could do to soften it up? It's not easy, is it? Sometimes warming up a cold heart feels downright impossible, especially when you're surrounded by so-called friends who keep letting you down. Ugh.

Think about this: God created you to be soft and tenderhearted toward people. It's not always easy, especially when you're exposed to so much mean-spiritedness in people around you. But don't give up on the truth that the Lord created you for tenderness. And remember, Jesus had to put up with a lot of hard-hearted people too, and He showed us that it is possible to keep on treating people tenderly.

Be kind to one another. Be thoughtful toward others. Care about the things others care about. Sense the pain of what they're going through. It's not easy, but it's so worth it.

Jesus, give me Your kind, compassionate heart toward everyone I meet today. Amen.

MORE LIFE-GIVING WORDS

"The Spirit alone gives eternal life. Human effort accomplishes nothing. And the very words I have spoken to you are spirit and life."
JOHN 6:63 NLT

What you say—to others and even to yourself—is very important. Don't believe it? Just ask Callie. She was bummed when she made a bad grade on a test. She started saying things like "I'm just a horrible student" and "I can't do this. I stink at science."

Those words stuck to her, and before long she was really struggling in class. Finally, her teacher had a talk with her. She explained that Callie was a good student. She just needed to start seeing herself that way.

From that day on, Callie started saying things like "I can do this! I can do all things through Christ who gives me strength!" She began to see an improvement in her attitude and in her grades.

Have you ever been like Callie? Do you catch yourself saying things like "I'm such a loser!" or "I'll never be able to do what other kids can do"? Those words are powerful. They plant themselves in your brain and your heart, and before long you start to believe them. God created you to speak life-giving words, girl, so begin to speak them today, and watch your situation change.

*I get it, Jesus! I need to speak life.
Help me, I pray. Amen.*

MORE GENTLENESS

But the Holy Spirit produces this kind of fruit in our lives: love, joy, peace, patience, kindness, goodness, faithfulness, gentleness, and self-control. There is no law against these things!
GALATIANS 5:22–23 NLT

What do you think of when you read the word *gentle*? Maybe you think of a mother gently cradling a baby in her arms or a dog owner tenderly patting his pooch on the head. To treat someone gently means you treat them with great care.

God created you to be gentle with others. Today's Bible verse proves that! You were made to produce the fruit of gentleness in your life. So what does that look like?

Imagine you're been given the task of carrying a single ostrich egg from one side of a football field to another. You'd handle it with gentleness, hands trembling all the way until you safely delivered it to its destination.

Now imagine you have a situation as delicate as that egg. It's going to require gentleness. Great care. You manage it just fine in part because you thought it through in advance. You made a decision to be gentle at any cost.

God designed you to be gentle—with your family, your teachers, your pets, even yourself. Decide today to handle yourself and those around you with greater care than ever before.

I'll be gentle, Jesus! I'll take care of the people You've placed in my life. They're more valuable to me than anything, so I'll treat them with love and kindness. Amen.

MORE STRENGTH TO THE POWERLESS

*He gives power to the weak and
strength to the powerless.*
Isaiah 40:29 nlt

You feel like a limp rag. If someone would just wring you out and hang you up to dry, that would be fine with you. You're done. . .with this day, with the people surrounding you, with that C you got on your science test, with your homework. . .everything. The exhaustion has taken hold to the point where nothing coming out of your mouth makes sense. All you want to do is take a hot bath and climb into bed.

We all have days where the exhaustion gets to us. Getting up early for school. Going to bed late because you're studying or working on a project. Emotional woes. Physical challenges. They threaten to rob us of that last bit of strength. But here's great news: God gives strength to the powerless. Not just any kind of strength, mind you, but supernatural strength. He gives power to the weak.

Picture the teensy-tiniest ant, suddenly muscular and strong enough to defend the whole colony. That's you, even when you don't feel like it. One drop of His strength and you're ready to tackle giants, even on days when you'd rather just curl up with a good book.

*Thank You for Your supernatural
strength, God! I really need it! Amen.*

MORE COMMITMENT

*Commit your work to the Lord,
and your plans will be established.*
Proverbs 16:3 esv

If you say you're going to do something, do you always follow through and do it? Some girls say, "Sure, I'll get to that later," or "I promise I'll be there." But when the time comes, they're nowhere to be found. They're off doing their own thing, completely oblivious to their commitment.

God made you to be a person who's committed. If you tell someone that you'll show up for an event, show up. If you tell your mom you'll (finally!) clean your room. . .clean your room. If you say, "I'll get that book read," read the book. It's not easy, especially with so many distractions, but you can do it if you'll stay committed.

God also calls you to be committed to your faith. It's not always easy to stick with your beliefs, especially with the world so off kilter, but it's critical to your survival! And He wants you to be committed to His Word as well, so don't forget to spend time in it and in prayer.

Finally, God designed you to be committed to others, especially those you care about. Give them your time, attention, and love—this is your service to them and to the Lord.

*I will check my commitment levels and do my best
to be more committed. . .with Your help, Jesus! Amen.*

MORE CAREFUL WITH YOUR LANGUAGE

Let no corrupting talk come out of your mouths, but only such as is good for building up, as fits the occasion, that it may give grace to those who hear.
EPHESIANS 4:29 ESV

She's on a roll. You wish you could stop her, but she doesn't even seem to notice the awful words spewing out of her mouth. Curse word after curse word. . .and she keeps going, like they're perfectly normal, good words.

Maybe you have a friend like this, one who uses language strong enough to make your hair curl. It can get old really quick, that's for sure! There's just something about what the Bible calls "coarse" language that brings down a conversation. And yet some people use that kind of language all the time, like it's absolutely nothing.

God made you for more than that, girl. He wants you to choose your words carefully, and not just when others are watching and listening. He's interested in what's inside your heart. And remember, Luke 6:45 (NLT) says, "What you say flows from what is in your heart." So if bad words are slipping out of your mouth, they're starting way down deep in your heart.

It's time to wave goodbye to curse words and other coarse language. Commit to purity, and you will bless the heart of God (and others).

Lord, I'll do my best not to talk like they talk. Guard my heart and my tongue, I pray. Amen.

MORE OKAY WITH BEING DIFFERENT

For we are his workmanship, created in Christ Jesus for good works, which God prepared beforehand, that we should walk in them.
EPHESIANS 2:10 ESV

You don't look like the other girls. You don't have the same interests as the other girls. You don't even talk like them. It's not like you're trying to stick out like a sore thumb. There are times when it would be easier to blend in. But you're uniquely. . .you. And that's okay! In fact, that's exactly how God made you to be.

So many girls spend their lives trying to look, act, and be like their friends. It's a futile game they play. No one can keep up with it. And why would you want to? Being like someone else isn't what you were created to do. The Lord designed you uniquely. You're one of a kind and rightfully so! So don't waste your time trying to fit in. Don't change your wardrobe, your hair, or your attitude in the hopes that they will suddenly include you in their clique. You'll set a far greater example to others if you remain true to yourself—in your attitude and actions and in the way you present yourself.

There's nothing wrong with just being you, girl. You're created in the image of God, after all, and He thinks you're pretty remarkable just the way you are.

Lord, I get it! You created me to be myself. I'm okay with that, even if it means I'm not like the other girls. I'm uniquely me, just who You made me to be. Amen.

MORE PROTECTION IN TIMES OF TROUBLE

*The Lord is a stronghold for the oppressed,
a stronghold in times of trouble.*
PSALM 9:9 ESV

Kenda's mom, dad, and sister all came down with the flu. She went from room to room, caring for them all, dishing out meds, bowls of soup, and lots and lots of hot tea. There was no one else to do it, and she didn't mind. It was nothing short of a miracle that she didn't end up sick herself.

Sometimes God does that—He physically protects you in times of danger. Other times He guards and protects your heart (from abusive words, from unkind language). The point is, God is your Protector. Whether you're walking out of a broken relationship or an unexpected tragedy with your family, He will be there to guard and protect.

The Lord has promised to be your Stronghold in times of trouble. When everything else is crumbling. . .He won't. When everyone else is running away, He stays put. You will go through hard times. There's no doubt about it. But your Protector will never leave your side.

*I trust You, my Protector. I'm so grateful
You are my Stronghold in times
of trouble, Lord! Amen.*

MORE JOY IN PLACE OF SORROW

"So also you have sorrow now, but I will see you again, and your hearts will rejoice, and no one will take your joy from you."
JOHN 16:22 ESV

It doesn't make sense. You've been through a tragedy. You should be reeling. Most girls would be. But you have this unexplainable sense of peace filling your heart. Yes, you're sad. Yes, your world has been rocked. But somehow, in the very midst of the pain, you've managed to find joy, the kind you never could have drummed up on your own.

God created you to have joy on good days and bad. Perhaps that's one reason laughter and tears are so closely connected. They hover near one another, each ready to activate as needed. And boy, does life ever give you opportunities to need them!

Don't ever be ashamed of your joy—even if it erupts in the middle of a rough season. It's a gift, after all, one you were born to enjoy.

I'm so grateful for the joy that fills my heart, Jesus! Sometimes it makes no sense. When my world is spinning out of control, I should be weeping. But many times You've stepped in and given me joy in place of mourning. I'm so grateful! Amen.

MORE LIKE JESUS IN YOUR THINKING

*For my thoughts are not your thoughts,
neither are your ways my ways, declares the Lord.*
ISAIAH 55:8 ESV

Dora stared at the picture of her mother that hung in the front hall of their house.

"You look like her, you know," her father said as he stepped next to her. "You always have. But now that you're a teen, I see the resemblance even more."

Dora saw it too. She and her mother almost looked like the same person!

The same is true of your relationship with God. He wants your thoughts to be so much like His that people can't tell you apart. All those heavy concerns can be lifted as you take on His thoughts.

So what areas do you need to work on? Where do you struggle in your thought life? Do you worry? Are you weighed down by self-consciousness? Are you overly anxious? Do you replay scenes or conversations in your head?

God can help you with all those things, but you have to give them to Him. He'll scrub those icky thoughts away and give you the mind of Christ. . .if you ask.

*Lord, You said in Your Word that You would
give me the mind of Christ. Today I'm asking for
that. No more dwelling on fretful thoughts. From
now on, I want to think like You, Jesus! Amen.*

MORE TASKS FINISHED

Keep his decrees and commands, which I am giving you today, so that it may go well with you and your children after you and that you may live long in the land the Lord your God gives you for all time.
Deuteronomy 4:40 niv

Remember that time you started a puzzle but gave up about halfway through it? And what about that time when you started a craft project but didn't finish it?

Nothing half-done is ever pretty to look at. A half-clean room isn't clean. A half-washed car isn't truly washed. A half-baked cake is just plain icky. A half-done job isn't done at all.

God created you to be a girl who finishes what she starts. Yep, that's right! It's a sloppy habit to start a bunch of things you never finish.

So how can you change that tendency? Start by having a good attitude. Example: You have a big project due for school. You have two weeks to complete it. You start out with a bang. It's going to be great. Then you give up about halfway into it. The night before it's due, you try to finish it, but it's just not turning out the way you had planned.

Jesus wants you to get that task done—not just for the sake of your grade, but to teach you that you—yes, you!—are a great finisher. That's what He created you to be, after all.

*I'll learn to be a good finisher,
Jesus. . .with Your help! Amen.*

MORE GOD-FOCUSED ROMANTIC DREAMS

But God shows his love for us in that while we were still sinners, Christ died for us.
ROMANS 5:8 ESV

All the girls are talking about him. You know the one. That boy in your English class. He's cute, he's just your age, and he seems to have a crush on you. Or does he? The other girls seem to think so, and they're a little jealous.

Maybe you don't spend a lot of time thinking about the opposite sex. . .or maybe you do. "Romance" is a big topic for many teen girls. Some of them are excited about the possibility of meeting Mr. Right. Of course, the chances of meeting your "Forever Mr. Right" while still in your teens is a bit iffy, but that doesn't stop some girls from trying.

God made you for God-focused romantic dreams. What does that mean, exactly? It means He longs for you to fall in love with Him first and to allow Him to show you what real romance is. It's a Savior who adores you, who wants to spend time with you, and who thinks you're the bomb!

Before you give your heart to a boy, make sure you're in the best possible relationship with your Savior. He has such big plans for you, and you don't want to miss out. So do your best to focus on Him for now. The rest can come later, in His perfect timing.

God, I will wait on You to meet the guy of my dreams. Right now I'm going to focus on spending more time with You! Thank You for loving me. Amen.

MORE HEALTHY GOALS

*Beloved, I pray that all may go well
with you and that you may be in good
health, as it goes well with your soul.*
3 JOHN 2 ESV

Working out. Choosing water instead of soda. Holding back on desserts. These are all things you know you should be doing, but why are they so hard?

Sure, you're busy. You have school, church, family, friends, and a ton of other things going on. But you're never too busy to take care of your health!

God created you to pay attention to the wonderful body He gave you. You're like the landlord of a beautiful house, and Jesus wants you to take good care of that house!

So what can you do to make sure you stay healthy? Start by getting enough sleep at night. (Yep, you read that right! It all starts with good sleep habits.) Next, pay a little more attention to what you're putting in your mouth. Maybe you eat too many sweets or drink too many sodas. It's time to mix it up and add some healthy options. Finally, get active! Lounging around on the sofa might seem fun at the time, but when you're tired, cranky, and putting on weight, it's not as much fun.

Take care of the vessel the Lord gave you, girl! He created you to live in it for a long, long time!

*I'll do a better job of taking care of me, Jesus.
Help me choose some healthy goals, I pray. Amen.*

MORE RESPECT FOR AUTHORITY

*Likewise, you who are younger, be subject to
the elders. Clothe yourselves, all of you, with
humility toward one another, for "God opposes
the proud but gives grace to the humble."*
1 PETER 5:5 ESV

You know you're supposed to respect authority. You've been told that all your life. But what does it mean exactly? And who does God count as authority figures in your life?

Think for a moment of all the people you have to answer to. Your parents. Teachers. The school principal. Police. These are all authority figures. But the elderly are also meant to be treated with great respect. Your grandparents, older people in your neighborhood and at church, and even those you meet in the store.

So what does "treating them with respect" look like? It starts with admitting that your parents, teachers, principal, and so on are the boss and you're not. They get the final say. It's up to them. (That's a hard pill to swallow, isn't it?) And it also means that you go out of your way to humbly submit yourself to their authority.

It's not easy to submit, but when you're the parent, you'll understand. When that day comes, you will hope and pray your kiddos treat you with the respect you deserve.

*I won't wait, Jesus! I'll start right now. . .today.
I'll treat my parents, grandparents, teachers,
and authorities with the respect they deserve. Amen.*

MORE HOPE FOR THE FUTURE

*There is surely a future hope for you,
and your hope will not be cut off.*
PROVERBS 23:18 NIV

You're a girl with a sense of purpose, and you have great hopes for your future. Okay, so you don't exactly know what's coming around the bend, but that doesn't bother you! You still bravely face the unknown because you trust God's plan for your tomorrows.

While others around you might be cowering in fear as life throws sour pickles their way, you lift your head high. Things might get tough, sure, but you're not giving up. You have hope, not just for the situations you're facing today, but for tomorrow as well.

You're expecting amazing things from the Lord, even if your circumstances are a little rough at the moment. But what if major troubles come your way? Will you give up then? Nope. You'll keep on keeping on. That's what hopeful girls do. They learn their lessons, square their shoulders, and keep moving forward, one day (and one foot) at a time.

*Lord, I'm a girl of hope. I know You designed
me this way. I place my trust, my hope,
my tomorrows in Your hands, Father. Amen.*

MORE PEACE WHEN YOU'RE FOCUSED ON HIM

"You keep him in perfect peace whose mind is stayed on you, because he trusts in you."
ISAIAH 26:3 ESV

Your friends are angry with each other, and you're stuck in the middle of their spat. Your teacher isn't happy with the project you just turned in. Mom isn't happy with the condition you left the kitchen in. The dog just threw up on the carpet.

Oh, and you? You're just about to lose it.

When you hit those points—when everything around you is spinning out of control—how do you respond? Do you hide in a closet and scream? Do you yell at your kid brother, thinking that one chance to holler at someone will solve all your problems at once?

God designed you to focus on Him in good times and bad. It's easier in good times, sure, but you sense His presence even more when you still your heart during tough seasons.

So take a deep breath, girl. Even now—right now, in the middle of the drama—you can be calm, cool, and collected.

Your peace is supernatural, Lord. That's why I depend on it so much! Thanks for giving it when I need it most. Amen.

MORE THAN CAST ASIDE

As you come to him, a living stone rejected by men but in the sight of God chosen and precious, you yourselves like living stones are being built up as a spiritual house.
1 Peter 2:4–5 esv

Kristin struggled with feelings of abandonment and rejection from the time she was in kindergarten. Being adopted by a loving family wasn't enough to get rid of the pain of rejection she felt. "Why did my birth mom give me up, anyway? Was I too much of a burden? Didn't she love me?" These questions always ran through her mind.

When Kristin got to her teens, she still battled those same feelings of being unwanted. She deliberately pushed her parents and siblings away, convinced they didn't really want her. It took the intervention of family members and the help of a great Christian therapist for Kristin to come to grips with the truth—she was more than her feelings of rejection.

Perhaps you've been rejected too. You've been cast aside by a parent, a group of friends, or even a boy you had a crush on. You're struggling with the "why" of it. Beautiful girl, God will never abandon you. You're His. . .forever. In His sight you are chosen and precious.

Lord, thank You for seeing me as precious in Your sight! I know You'll never reject me, Father. That truth brings deep joy. Amen.

MORE EMOTIONAL CONTROL

Whoever is slow to anger is better than the mighty, and he who rules his spirit than he who takes a city.
PROVERBS 16:32 ESV

Emotions. Everyone has them. And sometimes they get the better of you, don't they? So what do you do when they threaten to take over? You try to hold it all together, but some days it's just hard! You get so mad, you could spit! You get so emotional, you want to cry. You get so sad, you just want to lock yourself in your room and push the world away.

First of all, remember that God gave you those emotions, so don't be surprised when they show up. But He never meant for them to control you. He made you to be the one in control. It starts by taking a deep breath and asking Him to calm you down a bit. Then remember that you're not ruled by feelings. You're ruled by truth. And here's the truth: God in you is powerful enough to overcome your emotions. By yourself you can't do it, but with His help, you can.

Don't give in to fear. Don't give in to sadness. Don't give in to anger. Instead, rise above them. Lift your head and your heart and say these words: "Lord, I need Your help to overcome what I'm feeling!" He'll do it, you know.

Jesus, I really do need Your help if I'm going to be in control of my emotions and feelings. I can't do it by myself, and I don't want to. Help me, I pray! Amen.

MORE VICTORIES

You will walk upon the lion and the snake. You will crush under your feet the young lion and the snake.
Psalm 91:13 nlv

Hey, you—yes, you! Here's some fun (and exciting) news! You were created to be victorious! It's true. So don't just say "I'm a winner!" because all the cool kids are saying it. You really *are* a winner because God is fighting your battles through you.

Does that mean you'll win every single battle or come out on top in every single situation? Absolutely not. You'll learn more from your losses than your gains. And remember, character is formed in times of loss. But don't give up on being victorious, even when things don't go the way you hoped they would. Remember, your power comes from one place—Jesus Christ.

Here are several areas where the Lord wants you to triumph: He wants you to win the battle over sin. He wants you to triumph (be victorious) over addictions. He longs for you to triumph in your relationships. He wants you to triumph over any anger you might be feeling or any feelings of depression. And He's standing close by, loaded with the power to help you with all those things. You were made to be victorious, girl! Don't give up now.

I really am a victor in You, Lord! Thanks for giving me the courage to triumph. Amen.

MORE PERFECT LOVE

*For I am jealous for you with the jealousy
of God himself. I promised you as a pure
bride to one husband—Christ.*
2 CORINTHIANS 11:2 NLT

As a little girl, you probably dreamed of the perfect love story—of a prince on a white horse who would sweep in and carry you off to his magical kingdom where all your dreams would come true. (Hey, that's what all those fairy-tale movies make you think, right?)

Here's some terrific news, guaranteed to make your day: you can have the perfect fairy-tale romance! The hero in your story is Jesus, the lover of your soul. The Bible says that you are His bride. Wow, that's a cool thought. . .you're the bride of Christ!

No matter who you fall in love with (or who you marry), Jesus needs to be your first love. Always. Forever. No matter what. Second Corinthians 11:2 says that He's a jealous God. That means He wants your heart—totally and completely. When you put Him in His rightful place, everything else in your life will work out to His glory, and you will experience a perfect love, better than any fairy tale.

*I am Yours and You are mine, Lord!
I want to put You first in my life
and love You most! Amen.*

MORE WITH GOD ON YOUR SIDE

"And that all this assembly may know that the Lord saves not with sword and spear. For the battle is the Lord's, and he will give you into our hand."
1 SAMUEL 17:47 ESV

Ashton enjoyed a game of volleyball as well as the next girl, but she wasn't the best at the game. Oh, she gave it her best but could barely get the ball over the net, even on a good day.

Ashton especially loved when her older sister, Cherri, decided to play. Wow, was she good or what? With Cherri on the team, they would win every single game. Cherri brought star power. She awed players on both sides of the net, and there was never any question about which team would come out the victor.

That's what it's like when you realize God is on your side. He's got mad skills that even Cherri doesn't have. Folks all across the stadium cheer when the God of the universe takes His turn at serving the ball. *Whoosh!* He takes care of things in a hurry, doesn't He?

Jesus, I'm so glad You're on my side. You've got my back, even when others don't. And. . .wow! Do You ever shock my enemies! I'm so grateful when You intervene. Amen.

MORE WORTHY

So we keep on praying for you, asking our God to enable you to live a life worthy of his call. May he give you the power to accomplish all the good things your faith prompts you to do.
2 Thessalonians 1:11 nlt

"You are worthy in His sight."

What do you think of when you read those words? Do you feel worthy? Are you really, truly worthy when you stand before a holy and perfect God?

God created You in His image, and He's a holy, perfect God. You try hard to be perfect, but it's impossible. You just keep messing up, don't you? It's time to stop looking at yourself through the veil of "humanly perfection." You are made righteous (worthy) because of the blood of Jesus. When His blood was shed on the cross, He covered every bit of sin and shame you might ever experience. If you apply that blood to your life, it makes you worthy. Yes, it's true! You're worthy—because of Him.

Stop struggling with the "Am I good enough for God?" question. You're not. But through the blood of Jesus Christ. . .you are.

I get it! I'm really not worthy. I'm flawed and imperfect. But through Your blood, Jesus, all my sins are washed away, and I'm found worthy by You. Amen.

MORE CAREFUL WITH FOOD CHOICES

The temptations in your life are no different from what others experience. And God is faithful. He will not allow the temptation to be more than you can stand. When you are tempted, he will show you a way out so that you can endure.
1 CORINTHIANS 10:13 NLT

You're a growing girl, and the food choices out there are so tempting! Fries, sodas, burgers, milkshakes, ice cream sundaes. It's a feast for the eyes, isn't it?

Only one problem with all of that—most of those foods aren't very good for you. They might taste good, but they leave you feeling weak and sick if you have too much. There's not a lot of nutritional value in much of the food you see around you these days, which is sad.

God filled the earth with good foods for you to enjoy. There are so many healthy options. So the next time you're tempted to get that double cheeseburger, look at the menu and say, "I'm going to make a better choice." When you're at the ice cream parlor with your friends and you want a triple-decker cone, whisper the words, "Make a better choice." A lot of little choices will add up to a much healthier you!

Lord, I've struggled in this area, but I want to do better. You created me to make better food choices, and I don't always do my part. Help me make a better choice today, please! Amen.

MORE THAN A SOUR FACE

Be angry and do not sin; do not let the sun go down on your anger, and give no opportunity to the devil.
Ephesians 4:26–27 esv

It's hard to be around grumpy people. They sure can get on your nerves! They're never happy and always seem to be pointing out the bad in others without seeing it in themselves.

What about you? Would your friends say that you're grumpy or that you're usually laid back? No one likes a girl who goes around with a sour face all the time, like she's been eating pickles. That's such a turnoff! But everyone loves the girl who extends grace, mercy, and love even to those who've messed up.

God made you to be more than a sour face. He created you with forgiveness in your heart for others, and He enables you to show mercy to those who have hurt you. So don't get all wound up in your anger. Don't hyperfocus on the bad in those around you. Instead, spend more time praying for those people and offering them grace when they mess up. That's what you would want them to do for you. . .right?

*Lord, I need to learn to be more gracious
and merciful. I don't want to be a pickle face!
Help me not to be bitter or unforgiving, even
when I'm hurt. I want to show mercy, Father! Amen.*

MORE FAITH

But when you ask, you must believe and not doubt, because the one who doubts is like a wave of the sea, blown and tossed by the wind.
JAMES 1:6 NIV

"Do you have faith to believe?"

Jenna shook her head. "Not really, if you want the truth. Right now, I'm just not feeling it."

She wanted to believe that God could put her parents' marriage back together, but right now—with all the fighting going on in her house—that seemed absolutely impossible. No way, nohow could she imagine things working out. So why not give up now? What was the point in praying when the writing was on the wall?

Maybe you've walked a mile in Jenna's shoes. Things are so out of control that you think they'll never line up. Here's good news for you today: God can take any situation—even a chaotic one—and turn it around for the better. Unfortunately, this doesn't mean that having faith prevents negative things from happening in our lives. But it does mean that God will see us through.

Do you wonder sometimes why God doesn't just help the situation, whether you believe or not? He's wanting to activate your faith so that you can play a role in the miracle. (How exciting is that?)

So summon your faith. Get ready to watch God move! You were created for more faith, girl!

Lord, I'm ready! I'm so tired of living a faithless life. Show off, God! Make it big! And include me in the process as my faith is grown, I pray. Amen.

MORE BLESSINGS

The trustworthy person will get a rich reward, but a person who wants quick riches will get into trouble.
PROVERBS 28:20 NLT

Marigold got caught in a rainstorm just as she got off the school bus. Her house was a block away, and she didn't have an umbrella with her. Oh well. She'd just have to let the showers soak her and deal with the cleanup when she got home.

Sure enough, the rain had soaked her to the bone by the time she ran in the front door. Marigold glanced in the hallway mirror and laughed as she saw her reflection. "I look like a drowned rat."

Sometimes the rains come down and drench us like that. Other times, blessings fall at the same rate. We don't even see them coming (and certainly don't feel as if we deserve them), but they come regardless. They shower us and we're in heaven, wondering why.

God designed you to receive blessings, girl. He's poured out so many already, but plenty of surprises are yet to come. He wants to soak you in good things, much like the rain soaks you on a stormy day. Are you ready for those blessings? Ready or not, you'll be showered by them soon!

*Lord, I'm so grateful for Your many
blessings. I can count on You to shower
down wonderful things on me, Father. Amen.*

MORE LISTENING WITH YOUR HEART AND EARS

*Apply your heart to instruction and
your ears to words of knowledge.*
PROVERBS 23:12 NIV

Life always gives you opportunities to learn, whether you're in science class or hanging out at the mall with friends. It's so important to use your spiritual eyes and ears. Why? Because temptations are everywhere. But don't worry! If you keep those spiritual eyes and ears open wide, you can avoid the enemy's trap.

Why does it matter so much? Because there are some "friends" out there who want to pull you away from God. They want you to be like them, to do what they do and act like they act. They know your faith is getting in the way of that.

Don't fall for the devil's schemes! God is drawing you away from all that and toward Him. He has big stuff planned for you, so don't waste a minute following the wrong crowd.

Eyes wide open! Ears in tune. Pay attention and you'll go far. . .in the right direction!

*Lord, I'm listening! I won't be deceived by
so-called friends who want me to become
like them. I'll stick with You, Father, and do
what You've called me to do. Amen.*

MORE LOVE FOR NATURE

"But ask the animals, and they will teach you, or the birds in the sky, and they will tell you; or speak to the earth, and it will teach you, or let the fish in the sea inform you. Which of all these does not know that the hand of the Lord has done this? In his hand is the life of every creature and the breath of all mankind."
Job 12:7–10 niv

You can't help yourself. When you look at the ocean waves crashing on the shore, your heart just feels happy. And when you see mountains covered in fluffy white snow, you're blown away. Even the sight of a playful puppy makes you smile.

You're a nature lover, and that's a good thing! It just means you're enjoying God's beautiful creation. Those birds in the sky? He made them for your enjoyment! That river rushing over the rocks? He crafted that too.

The book of Genesis says that the Spirit of God moved over all of creation. So don't be surprised if you sense the Spirit when you're enjoying a long walk down scenic trails or a hike up the side of a mountain. You're feeling the breath of God as you enjoy His beautiful creation. He made you to love it, girl! So what are you waiting for? Get out there and enjoy this day!

I love the things You've made, Lord! Thank You for creating me to enjoy them. Amen.

MORE RESTED

*"Come to me, all you who are weary
and burdened, and I will give you rest."*
MATTHEW 11:28 NIV

Frazzled. That was the only word Veronica could think of to describe how she felt most of the time. Frazzled. Worn out. Exhausted. Between school, homework, volleyball, and chores, she barely had time to sleep, let alone take a day for herself. Before long, her body crashed. She ended up sick and was forced to take a few days off, whether she wanted to or not.

God created your body to rest. He created the Sabbath because He knew mankind would want to keep going, even past the breaking point. If you really take time off—to relax, recharge, and renew—you'll get more work done. If you don't take the time to rest, you'll eventually collapse. Things won't look pretty.

Say these words to yourself and mean them: "God created me to rest more!"

Whew! Doesn't that feel amazing?

*I've been so tired, Lord. But You see,
You understand, and You're here to help me
get the rest I need. Thank You, Father. Amen.*

MORE OF A GODLY WORLDVIEW

*Do not be conformed to this world, but be
transformed by the renewal of your mind,
that by testing you may discern what is the will
of God, what is good and acceptable and perfect.*
ROMANS 12:2 ESV

Let's face it: most people don't see things the way you do. If you're a Christian, you have what's called a "Christian worldview." That means you try to see things that are going on through the eyes of Jesus. When someone hurts you, you try to reconcile and offer forgiveness. When people get sick, you pray for them. When bad things are happening in your community, like a hurricane or a wildfire, you band together with others and do what you can to help your neighbors. That's what believers do.

But not everyone believes in Jesus. Their worldview isn't like yours. They're not quick to forgive. They put themselves first. They don't seem to notice when they've hurt others. It's hard to be around these people, for sure.

Don't give up on those with a different worldview, girl! Keep praying for them to come to know Christ so that their eyes will be opened too.

*Lord, I won't give up! I'll keep seeing people
through Your eyes! I won't change my worldview
or my ways to please them, but I'll pray that they
change as they come to know You. Amen.*

MORE CONFIDENCE

Let us then with confidence draw near to the throne of grace, that we may receive mercy and find grace to help in time of need.
HEBREWS 4:16 ESV

Geneva struggled with a real lack of confidence. It started when she was a little girl. She didn't get a lot of encouragement from her parents or teachers, especially at school. She wasn't the best student. Ugh. And her grades didn't seem to get any better when she got into middle school. The best she could pull off were Bs and Cs.

That wasn't the only area where Geneva struggled. She couldn't help but compare herself to others. Was she as pretty as that girl? Was she as popular as the other one? Would she ever measure up or always be found lacking?

God never intended His girls to play the comparison game. He wants your confidence to be rooted not in your own abilities or looks but in Him.

Ask God to show you how to overcome your lack of confidence and to turn your gaze to Him. He's the confidence booster, the One you can trust for a jolt of heavenly assurance. You were created for more of His confidence, girl!

*Lord, I trust in Your confidence, not my own.
I draw near today because I know You'll
help me. What I cannot do alone, You can
do through me. I'm so grateful! Amen.*

MORE MOUNTAINS MOVED

"You don't have enough faith," Jesus told them. "I tell you the truth, if you had faith even as small as a mustard seed, you could say to this mountain, 'Move from here to there,' and it would move. Nothing would be impossible."
MATTHEW 17:20 NLT

Obstacles. April saw nothing but obstacles in her way. They loomed like mountains, stretching to the sky in front of her, casting terrifying shadows down below. She shivered with fear as she gazed up at them.

Relationship mountains—more friend drama than she could take.

Mountains of loss—after the unexpected death of her grandmother.

Mountains of confusion—after hearing that her parents might be splitting up.

Perhaps you've faced mountains like April's. You've stared at them completely defeated, convinced you'll never get past them.

God created you to be more than a shadow dweller when mountains rise up in the path before you. You can speak to those mountains and watch them disappear into the sea!

Summon your faith, girl! Open your mouth. . .and speak!

Lord, today I speak to the mountains in my life. You created me to do it, and I trust Your plan. Mountains, be gone in the mighty name of Jesus! Amen.

MORE CHEER

*Rejoice in the Lord always;
again I will say, rejoice.*
PHILIPPIANS 4:4 ESV

You see those cheerleaders out on the football field. They're dressed in their cute little outfits, jumping up and down with pom-poms in hand. They holler out fun chants to get the fans excited about the game. They're bubbly and fun, as long as the game is going on. Afterward, maybe not so much!

What about you? Are you the bubbly sort? Do you always want to holler out things to encourage people and lift their spirits? Are you the girl everyone goes to when they're hurting because they know you'll make them feel better? If so, great! There's nothing better than being a cheerleader for Jesus. In fact, He created you to be filled with joy—to the point where your joy spills over onto others.

So don't hide your joy, girl! Spread it from person to person, situation to situation. Be the sweet one. Be the loving one. Be the joyful one. Who knows? You just might change the world!

*Lord, I want to be a cheerleader for You.
Help me to remain filled with joy, even on
the hard days, so that I can lift the spirits
of others who are hurting. Amen.*

MORE PHYSICALLY FIT

*Don't you realize that your body is the temple of the
Holy Spirit, who lives in you and was given to you by God?
You do not belong to yourself, for God bought you with
a high price. So you must honor God with your body.*
1 CORINTHIANS 6:19–20 NLT

You know you should do it. You should take better care of yourself. You should spend more time walking, soaking up the sunshine, or getting involved in sports. And yes, you should probably cut back on some of the sweets and fried foods, replacing them with healthier options. God created you to be physically fit, after all.

But why? Why does it matter to Him?

Take a closer look at today's Bible verse. Your body— no matter how tall, how short, how chubby, how thin—is a temple for the Holy Spirit. Think about that for a moment. It's like a jar you might pour milk into, a vessel to "hold" the Spirit of God.

Whoa. Does the Spirit of God want to live in a broken-down house? Of course not! That's why the verse goes on to say that you should honor God with your body. You have to be in the best shape possible to have a houseguest as important as the Holy Spirit.

Is it time to make some changes today? Pray about it; then offer your body to God.

*Lord, my body is Yours! Thank You for living inside of me!
I will do my best to take care of this temple. Amen.*

MORE SPEAKING UP

So the king gave the order, and they brought Daniel and threw him into the lions' den. The king said to Daniel, "May your God, whom you serve continually, rescue you!"
DANIEL 6:16 NIV

Poor Daniel. Thrown into the lions' den for sticking up for his faith. Can you even imagine? Sounds scary, right? God rescued Daniel from the lions' den. Whew! It was surely a terrifying experience, but he survived it.

Maybe you know what it feels like to be persecuted (ridiculed, hurt) for your faith. When you stand up for what you believe, sometimes people turn on you. Maybe they don't like your opinions or don't want to hear what the Bible says about a tough topic. You can't let that stop you.

Chances are pretty good you won't be thrown into a real lions' den if you speak up about what you believe. But if you ever *do* find yourself in a rough spot, don't fret! God will rescue you just as He rescued Daniel. He's got your back, girl!

Whew! Being a Christian is tough sometimes, Lord. People want me to keep my mouth shut and not talk to them about You. But how can I stop, Jesus? I'll go on sharing, and I'll count on You to rescue me. Amen.

MORE FUN HOBBIES

So I decided there is nothing better than to enjoy food and drink and to find satisfaction in work. Then I realized that these pleasures are from the hand of God.
ECCLESIASTES 2:24 NLT

If you're like most teen girls, you love to do stuff other than just schoolwork. (Let's face it: life can be a bit of a drag if all you do is work, work, work!) Here are some fun things you might enjoy: singing. Acting. Dancing. Painting. Sketching. Playing sports. Volunteering. Leading a Bible study. Playing an instrument. It's those "extras" that make life even more fun!

God made you to enjoy life and to develop your skills in a variety of areas. Cooking. Baking. Sewing. Calligraphy. Coin collecting. Crocheting. Puzzles. Reading. Dog training. These are just a few of the possibilities. A few others might include fashion design, makeup artistry, hairstyling, and jewelry making.

So what sounds good to you? What hobbies would you like to try? Remember, it takes twenty-one days to form a habit, so don't give up after only one or two. Keep at it. Develop your skills. Learn something new, and then teach it to others so they can enjoy it too.

Lord, I love the idea of trying something new and fun. Lead me in the right direction, I pray. Amen.

MORE FAMILY FOCUSED

God sets the lonely in families, he leads out the prisoners with singing; but the rebellious live in a sun-scorched land.
Psalm 68:6 niv

Sometimes they get on your nerves, but you know you love 'em. Those parents. Those siblings. Those aunts, uncles, grandparents, cousins, and distant relatives. Sure, they're chaotic and a little crazy at times. They certainly fill your life with adventure (and drama). But you wouldn't have it any other way! That's because God designed you to be family focused.

Have you ever wondered why the Lord placed people into families? Today's verse gives you the answer. Without a family unit, people would get lonely. They would have no one to talk things over with. No shoulders to cry on. No one to reason things out with. Without a family, you wouldn't have the support you need to make it through the big stuff. They're your cheerleaders, after all!

That's what God wants you to be for them too. Being more family focused means you care when that brother or sister is hurting. You want to make things better, not worse. You guard. You protect. You love ferociously! (That means you love even when you'd rather fight.)

God placed you in your family for a reason, so be the best family member you can be!

Lord, thank You for placing me in a family. I want to love them more, to care more deeply about the things that matter to those I love. Help me, I pray. Amen.

MORE SECURITY

*He drew me up from the pit of destruction,
out of the miry bog, and set my feet upon
a rock, making my steps secure.*
PSALM 40:2 ESV

What does it mean to be secure? A house is secure when the windows and doors are shut and locked. But surely God isn't asking you to lock yourself up like a house or a car!

Take a look at what today's verse says about security. If God saved you (and He did), then He must have saved you from something. From what, you ask? From sin. Bad habits. Grumpy attitudes. Selfish behaviors. And when He saved you, He set your feet upon a rock (hint: He's the Rock!), and He made your feet secure.

Think of it this way. If you're dragging your feet through deep sand at the beach, it's tough to walk. You don't feel secure. (You certainly couldn't do it in heels!) But once you hit solid ground (concrete). . .whew! You're safe and sound. You're secure.

God made you to be secure in Him, so turn your back on sin and stand firm on the Rock, Jesus. Don't give in to temptation. Stand firm, even if others around you are sinking in the sand!

*Jesus, thank You for putting my feet on the Rock!
I'm tired of stumbling and falling. No matter what's
happening around me, I'm sticking close to You
so that I'm safe and secure. Amen.*

MORE FOCUS ON WHAT MATTERS

*Keep your heart with all vigilance,
for from it flow the springs of life.*
PROVERBS 4:23 ESV

If someone asked you, "What matters most in your life?" how would you answer? Some might say, "My family." Others might say, "My friends." Still others might say, "My grades, because I want to get into a great college."

How you feel about what matters is important, because you give your time, talent, and energies to the things that matter to you. But God designed you to focus more on the things that matter to Him. (It's not that He doesn't care about what matters to you; it's just that He has big plans for you!)

So what matters to God? Loving others as you love yourself. Growing your faith. Sharing the Gospel (telling others about Him). Using your gifts to expand His kingdom.

Can you see now that what matters to you and what matters to Him might actually overlap? You love your family. . .and He wants you to love them even more! You care about your grades; He wants you to give your talents (academics, the arts. . .whatever) to Him.

Focus on what matters to Him, and before long it will matter to you too!

*Lord, I get it. You love me, and You're glad I have
things that matter. But when I focus on what
matters to You, we both win! I'm so grateful. Amen.*

MORE ATTENTION TO DETAILS

*Therefore we must pay much closer attention
to what we have heard, lest we drift away from it.*
HEBREWS 2:1 ESV

"I told you to clean your room."

You stare at your mom, surprised at her words, and then respond, "I *did* clean my room."

"You did? Really? Let's look again." She points out the laundry thrown onto the chair in the corner and a couple of dishes on the bedside table. Then she mentions the floor that needs vacuuming and dresser that needs tidying.

Really? You have to do all of *that* before she considers it clean?

Here's the thing: God created you to pay more attention to details. If you're not careful with the little things now, imagine how hard it's going to be when you get older and have to do things like cooking (following recipes), driving (keeping up with all the other traffic on the road), and taking care of a newborn (meeting their every need around the clock). Whew! That sounds like a lot of work.

It's your attention to detail that shows you care. That's why you get good grades on school projects you work extra hard on. Your attention to detail shows, and the teacher rewards you.

What areas of your life do you need to examine more closely? Pay attention to the details, and God will reward you.

*I'll pay more attention to the
little things, Lord, I promise! Amen.*

MORE RE-

Return, Israel, to the LORD your God. Your sins have been your downfall! Take words with you and return to the LORD. Say to him: "Forgive all our sins and receive us graciously, that we may offer the fruit of our lips."
HOSEA 14:1–2 NIV

Maybe you're a little puzzled by the title of today's devotion. What does *Re-* mean, anyway? *Re-* is a prefix, and you see it a lot in many familiar words. Here are just a few: Repeat. Return. Rerun. Renovate. When you *re-* something, you do it again. You get a do-over.

Take a close look at today's verse. God longs for His kids to repent and return. And He made you to *re-* too! Redo when you make a mistake. Repent when you've messed up. Return to Him, no matter what you've done. Remember His love. Repeat your promises to Him.

God is in the *re-* business. He loves to offer do-overs. So what's holding you back? If you're in a place where you need a second chance, just *re-*dedicate your heart and life to Him.

Father, I get it! You made me for the re-! Today I choose to repent and return to You. Please forgive me for my mess-ups! Thank You for giving me the chance to recommit myself to You. Amen.

MORE HELPFUL ATTITUDE

*Do nothing out of selfish ambition or vain conceit.
Rather, in humility value others above yourselves,
not looking to your own interests but each
of you to the interests of the others.*
Philippians 2:3–4 niv

"Ugh. I don't feel like it."

"But I need your help, honey."

"Can't you ask someone else?"

Maybe you've had one of those conversations with your mom. Or your teacher. They need help, but you're preoccupied with a video game. Don't they see you're busy?

Here's the truth: God made you to be more helpful. You might read that and say, "Whoa! I didn't sign up for this when I became a Christian. You mean I have to do more than I already do?"

It's not just a matter of doing more—it's having the right attitude or heart reaction to the needs of others. If your mom needs you to do the dishes, it shouldn't become an argument. Your heart needs to align with God's at that moment so that you can see what a blessing it will be to your mom if you quickly do what she's asked.

What will it take to change your attitude so that you're responsive to the needs of others? Today, spend some time in prayer. Ask God a simple question: "Who needs my help?" and then help that person.

*Lord, I'm tired of fighting over the things
I don't feel like doing. From now on, I want
to be a more thoughtful helper. Amen.*

MORE UNSEARCHABLE THINGS

"Call to me and I will answer you and tell you great and unsearchable things you do not know."
JEREMIAH 33:3 NIV

McKinsey wasn't sure who to go to with the big questions: "Why do bad things happen to good people?" "Why does God allow sickness and pain in this life?" "Why is Jesus the only way to heaven?" She was filled with questions like these and eventually found a friend from church who helped her discover the answers in the Bible.

Maybe you're struggling to find answers to life's deeper questions too. You're wondering some of the same things McKinsey is. Search the Word of God, and you'll find verse after verse to shed light on most of your questions, of course, but also don't forget to go directly to the Lord. He's not afraid of your tough questions. He doesn't get offended or upset if you say, "I don't get it, Lord. Why did You allow this (or that) to happen?" He's gentle enough to whisper His responses in your ear, all the while bringing comfort to your heart.

The Lord made you to call on Him. He longs to tell you great and unsearchable things. But first. . .you have to ask. What will you ask Him today?

Lord, today I'll start with this question. . .[fill in the blank].

MORE SUBMISSION

*Trust in the Lord with all your heart and lean not on
your own understanding; in all your ways submit
to him, and he will make your paths straight.*
PROVERBS 3:5–6 NIV

"More of you, less of me." Nina spoke the words aloud. More of the Lord meant more time submitting to His will, His way. She had to stop trying to fix her problems in the usual way; now she had to wait on Him for the perfect solution.

If you're like Nina, you're not a fan of waiting on God. (Let's face it—what girl is?) And submitting to His perfect will during the waiting? No fun. Still, that's what He wants you to do.

Why? Because the Lord wants to make sure you fully trust Him. When He's convinced you're looking to Him and not yourself, He's free to move.

Submission isn't a bad word. To submit just means you bow to His authority. And isn't that the ultimate goal, really—for His authority to reign?

*Lord, I submit to Your authority even as I'm
waiting for the answers I seek. I know I can trust You
because of Your deep love for me, Father. So I'm here,
heart open and head bowed, while I wait. Amen.*

MORE OF HIM, LESS OF YOU

"Seek the Kingdom of God above all else, and live righteously, and he will give you everything you need."
MATTHEW 6:33 NLT

Commercials say it, Hollywood makes a big deal about it, and even schools teach it: self comes first. Whatever self wants, self gets. Whatever self craves, self should have! (Hey, you probably have friends who really believe this!)

This is the opposite of what God's Word says, of course! To have more of Him, we really need to have less of ourselves.

What does this look like in the real world? Less of you and more of Him means you have to sacrifice a little sleep time and actually go to that before-school Bible study you promised you'd attend. It means you have to swallow hard and not bite back when someone snaps at you. (Ouch!)

Saying no to self means caring more about others than yourself. (As an example, remember when you were little and your mama made fried chicken, and you always insisted on the thigh piece? It's time to let that go now. Give that thigh to someone else, girl. You take the leg. It's just as tasty.)

Less of you. It's not always easy, but it's always right if you want more of Him.

Today I offer You all of me, Lord, so that I might die to self and live to worship You. Amen.

MORE MEMORIES

This is what I have observed to be good: that it is appropriate for a person to eat, to drink and to find satisfaction in their toilsome labor under the sun during the few days of life God has given them—for this is their lot.
ECCLESIASTES 5:18 NIV

Going on vacation with your family. Having a blast at a slumber party with your friends. Singing in your pajamas with your kid sister. These are the kinds of memories you'll be able to look back on and smile about.

God created you to have wonderful memories. So take snapshots in your mind (or on your phone) when you're enjoying yourself so that you never forget. Another way to remember those memories is to journal about them. Write down the experience, sharing all the details. Then, years from now, you can go back and read about it.

Why do you think the Lord cares about making memories? Because He created you to enjoy life! Today's verse says it's appropriate (good) for a person to find satisfaction in their labor. So when you're able to take a break from schoolwork, chores, and other tasks, make a few memories. (And remember, it's also possible to make memories while you're working! You'll remember those fondly too.)

Lord, I want to have wonderful memories. Thank You for reminding me to take snapshots in my mind and to write down the fun things I get to do so that I never forget. Amen.

MORE FOCUS ON WHAT JESUS DID FOR YOU

For the message of the cross is foolishness to those who are perishing, but to us who are being saved it is the power of God.
1 CORINTHIANS 1:18 NIV

Bridgette came to know the Lord as a little girl. She gave her heart totally and fully to Him, accepting Jesus as Savior and King of her heart. From that moment on, she did her best to live for Him.

When she got to middle school, Bridgette got involved in a lot of church activities. She joined the youth group. Then she joined the teen choir and offered to help the director. She stayed busy, busy, busy. If you had said, "Tell me about your faith," she probably would have filled your ears with stories of all the stuff she did at church but little about her faith journey. It took second place to her busyness.

Maybe you're in the same boat. You're super active at your church. You can't seem to remember where your salvation leaves off and your church busyness begins.

Maybe it's time to take a breath and examine those two things as two separate things. You were made to focus on what Jesus did to change your life, after all!

Lord, I love my church and enjoy the busyness, but may I never forget the work You've done in my heart! I'm forever grateful. Amen.

MORE DURING THE GOOD TIMES

Whatever is good and perfect is a gift coming down to us from God our Father, who created all the lights in the heavens. He never changes or casts a shifting shadow.
JAMES 1:17 NLT

Have you ever felt guilty when things were going right? Maybe you've had hard seasons. Then a blissful one comes. You're doing well in school. Things are going great with your BFF. You're getting along with Mom and Dad. Everyone in the family is healthy. And, for whatever reason, you start feeling awkward about the fact that things are okay. You look around and notice the friend who's going through cancer, and you're feeling guilty that you are healthy. You see that friend whose grandmother just passed away, and you feel guilty because you're about to go on a vacation with your grandma.

God wants you to enjoy the good seasons, sister! Even those people you're fretting over want you to celebrate the blissful times. If they could say anything to you right now, it might be: "Girl! You think I want you to suffer just because I'm suffering? You think I want you unhappy just because I'm unhappy?"

Pray for those in need. Take care of them. Send cards. Give hugs. Show up. But don't sacrifice your joy. It won't make their situation any better.

*Lord, thank You for all the seasons—
the good and the bad. Amen.*

MORE DURING THE TOUGH TIMES

"So when all these things begin to happen, stand and look up, for your salvation is near!"
LUKE 21:28 NLT

Brittany wasn't ready for catastrophe to hit. The nation was under a quarantine due to a virus, and she was caught off guard. She got completely freaked out whenever she watched the news. She was even more scared when she had to go out in public. All around her, neighbors and friends were gathering food and other essentials as if the world were coming to an end. It was almost more than she could handle!

Perhaps you've reacted like Brittany during a crisis. You want to shut off the news and pretend everything's normal. God wants you to be prepared for tough times—whether they involve the loss of a loved one, sickness, or a pandemic!

Jesus will give you all you need during the tough seasons. More faith. More hope. More joy. More kindness to others. He will help you be more of a blessing to those in need. More dedicated to spreading the Word.

Tough times will come. . .but you will soar because of the "more."

Lord, I have to admit, hard times make me nervous. But I choose to trust You. I was made for more than troubles. Thank You for that reminder. Amen.

MORE TIME WITH OTHER CHRISTIANS

*Not neglecting to meet together, as is the
habit of some, but encouraging one another,
and all the more as you see the Day drawing near.*
HEBREWS 10:25 ESV

"I'm so busy." Anita's nose wrinkled as she spoke. "I just don't have time to join a Bible study or go to youth group. I'm so overloaded with schoolwork and sports that I barely make it to church on Sunday mornings."

Maybe you can relate to Anita's explanation. You're busy too. You have so much going on—in school and out! Making the time to spend with other Christians is hard, even though you have tried.

Oh, but you need to keep trying! The more you hang out with other believers, the stronger you'll get. The Lord designed you to spend more time with His kids, after all. If you go too long without them, you'll grow weak. So stop with the excuses! Do what you can to hang out with friends who love Jesus. You'll be so glad you did.

*I need more time with my church family, Lord!
No more excuses. I'm going to show up and
link arms with those around me. Amen.*

MORE SPIRITUAL GROWTH

*Anyone who lives on milk cannot
understand the teaching about
being right with God. He is a baby.*
HEBREWS 5:13 NLV

Babies grow and change a lot over the first couple of years! Don't believe it? Check out pictures from when you were an infant! One minute you were dressed in newborn clothes that were still too big; the next a size four diaper was too small.

Babies grow. . .and grow. . .and grow. That's why your mom and dad took a lot of pictures—because they were afraid they'd forget what you looked like at each stage. The days seem to sail by!

God wants to see you grow too, once you give your heart to Him. Like that baby girl, you need to "change sizes" as the days, weeks, months, and years go by. He wants you to grow and develop in your faith, to have such a lasting change in attitude, spirit, and wisdom that people can barely remember what you were like before. It's time to stop living on milk, girl, and head for the meat and potatoes of His Word.

*Lord, I'm ready to grow up in You. I want to
be all You long for me to be, Father. Amen.*

MORE LOVE FOR PEOPLE WHO ARE HURTING

*Bear one another's burdens,
and so fulfill the law of Christ.*
GALATIANS 6:2 ESV

They're all around you. The mother whose child just passed away. The grandmother who sits alone in her home, forgotten by family members. The girl in your math class, ridiculed by her so-called friends. The man sleeping under the bridge. The little boy who's being abused by his dad.

The world is filled with broken people wishing they could be made whole again. They need friends like you, friends who have a heart for the broken and wounded.

The reason your heart quickens when you see that young mom with no groceries for her kids is because God put His heart inside of you. The reason it hurts so much when you find out a local child has been abused is because God's heart—beating inside of you—is broken. You were born for this, sweet girl. Caring for others is as important to you as breathing, and it warms the heart of God.

*I want to do what I can to help others
who are broken, Lord. Lead me, day by day,
to the ones who need me most. Amen.*

MORE DOERS OF THE WORD

*Do not merely listen to the word,
and so deceive yourselves. Do what it says.*
JAMES 1:22 NIV

She sat in church every Sunday, heard every message, could even quote the lines of the worship songs and some of the scriptures the pastor used. But as soon as fifteen-year-old Traci was outside the walls of the church, none of it really mattered to her. She lived like she wanted, dated who she wanted, ran around with the friends she wanted. In other words, she heard the Word. . .but didn't do it.

God wants you to be a doer, not just a hearer. It's not enough to show up for church, youth group, and church camp. It means nothing to memorize verses for the Bible quiz, invite the pastor over for lunch, or sit through a thousand services if the messages aren't penetrating your heart. Yes, those are good things, but a doer of the Word really takes to heart what she's heard. She changes her attitude, her thinking, the way she treats others. She accepts Jesus—way down deep in her heart.

Are you a hearer. . .or a doer? Only you can answer that question. But remember—you were created to be a doer.

*I want to follow through. I want to
be more than a hearer, but I'm going
to need Your help, Jesus! Amen.*

MORE LIGHT FOR YOUR PATH

*Your word is a lamp for my feet,
a light on my path.*
PSALM 119:105 NIV

Courtney had always been told that eyes adjusted to the darkness. Stumbling across the pitch-dark bedroom one night, she wasn't so sure. And when she caught her toe on the edge of the bed frame, she *really* wasn't sure! So much for adjusting!

The truth is, we all need light to guide our path. Stumbling around in the dark is no fun, whether you're in a dark room at night or on a journey down life's highway.

The tiniest bit of light can point out bumps in the road, snakes slithering along your path, or even broken pavement.

God's Word is the light you need to guide your path toward Him. It brightens the path ahead of you and gives you wisdom, peace, and more guidance than your mom or dad's GPS system. You were designed for more of that heavenly glow, girl! You were created to follow that light and to trust His plan, even in unfamiliar places.

Let Jesus be your Guide. You'll be so glad you took the journey!

*Shine that light bright, Lord! I don't
want to miss it. I'll follow Your
lead in all things. Amen.*

MORE HUMILITY

*Pride goes before destruction,
a haughty spirit before a fall.*
PROVERBS 16:18 NIV

A lot of girls think they're "all that and a bag of chips." Hey, you might even get like that yourself sometimes. It's not that you're deliberately trying to be prideful. But when someone compliments you—on your sports ability, your singing, your grades, the way you look—you can't seem to help yourself. You try to respond in humility, but somehow you often end up saying something prideful in response.

God didn't make you to be a bragger, girl! It's great when others brag about you, but when you start pointing the spotlight at yourself. . .watch out! The Lord made you to have humility, and that means you have to see the talents in others before you puff yourself up! Remember: Jesus loves a humble heart.

*Lord, I get it. You created me to be humble.
Help me get over myself! I want to think
more of others and less of myself. Amen.*

MORE TRUSTING IN THE SILENCE

*"The Lord will fight for you,
and you have only to be silent."*
Exodus 14:14 esv

She prayed for months. Then she prayed some more. But Aria didn't get any answer at all from the Lord. Not a *"Wait,"* not a *"No,"* not even an *"I hear you."* The Almighty seemed silent. . .and that really bothered her. Did He not care about what she was going through? After a while, she gave up praying altogether. What good was it doing?

There really are seasons of silence from the Lord. No doubt you've been through them. You wonder if He's truly listening or if He even knows you're pouring out your heart to Him.

Sweet girl, you were made to trust more in the silence. This is where your faith is sharpened. It's easy to exhibit trust when you clearly hear the Lord's voice, but when all you hear is crickets chirping, that's the most important time of all to hang on. When the silence is over, His voice will come breaking through loud and clear!

*Lord, I choose to trust You, even in the silence.
I don't always know what You're up to, but I
continue to place my trust in You. Amen.*

MORE UNITY

I appeal to you, brothers and sisters, in the name of our Lord Jesus Christ, that all of you agree with one another in what you say and that there be no divisions among you, but that you be perfectly united in mind and thought.
1 CORINTHIANS 1:10 NIV

Divisions between Christians can be awful! There's nothing worse than realizing you're in the middle of a split between friends. Ouch. Talk about painful. (And where do you place your loyalties when friends are divided? What a mess!)

God created His children to be unified. It's not easy, but it's the only way to keep His kids working in power. When divisions are created (and let's face it—they're way too common), you're not as effective, and neither are the other people involved. You grow weak, and that's just what the enemy of your soul—Satan—wants!

The body of Christ was never meant to be weak. Neither were you. So, to the best of your ability, remain unified with other believers. It's not always easy, but it will keep you all strong.

Lord, thank You for the body of Christ.
I want to be unified with other Christians
so that Your power will flow! Amen.

MORE STRENGTH TO SAY NO

Furious with rage, Nebuchadnezzar summoned Shadrach, Meshach and Abednego. So these men were brought before the king, and Nebuchadnezzar said to them, "Is it true, Shadrach, Meshach and Abednego, that you do not serve my gods or worship the image of gold I have set up?"
DANIEL 3:13–14 NIV

You know it goes against everything you believe. You know it will break God's heart. And if your parents find out, it will break their hearts too. But the temptation is really getting to you. You are crazy tempted to do the wrong thing. Something big. Something you've never tried before. You just can't seem to help yourself!

Wait! Don't you know that God made you strong so that you could resist temptation? It's true! And here's a hard truth no one tells you: if you give in to the pressure now, things will get harder as you get older. A few drinks now could lead to becoming an alcoholic later on. Smoking cigarettes could lead to a painful addiction. . .possibly even death. Giving away your sexual purity could lead to a lifetime of struggles.

Sin seems so innocent in the moment of temptation, but if you could see into the future, if you only knew the price you'll pay for bowing down now, you would definitely steer clear.

God gave you strength to say no. Don't. Bow. Down.

Okay, Lord, I get the message. I won't bow down to the temptation in front of me. Today—thanks to You—I'm strong enough to say no!

MORE TRIALS INTO TRIUMPHS

Consider it pure joy, my brothers and sisters, whenever you face trials of many kinds, because you know that the testing of your faith produces perseverance. Let perseverance finish its work so that you may be mature and complete, not lacking anything. If any of you lacks wisdom, you should ask God, who gives generously to all without finding fault, and it will be given to you.
JAMES 1:2–5 NIV

Penni wasn't sure why she had so many trials (problems) in her life. One friend said it must be because of something she'd done. . .somehow she must have brought the pain on herself. She found these words cruel, especially since she'd been a Christian since she was a little girl and always tried to live a godly life.

It didn't seem fair that catastrophe after catastrophe happened, but at the end of each one, Penni was always able to share some sort of testimony of how God had come through for her.

Maybe you've gone from tragedy to triumph, like Penni. Maybe you've been in the middle of a horrible event when the Lord stepped in and turned the mess into a message.

God created you to have more "trial to triumph" stories. He doesn't intend for you to be struggling all the time. Remember, you have a very real enemy out there, and he is out to steal, kill, and destroy. You can overcome him, though, when you take authority in the name of Jesus!

Lord, thank You for the many times You've turned my trials into triumphs and my problems into praise! Amen.

MORE AGREEMENT

Tell your people about these things again. In the name of the Lord, tell them not to argue over words that are not important. It helps no one and it hurts the faith of those who are listening.
2 Timothy 2:14 NLV

Arguments. They happen, whether you want them to or not. You say one thing; your friend says another. You believe one thing; your friend believes something else. It's hard, especially when accusations start flying.

So how does God expect you to have more agreement in your dis-agreements? First, look at that prefix *dis-*. It means "apart" or "away." When you're in disagreement with someone (Mom, Dad, a teacher, your friend, etc.), the enemy of your soul is trying to push you away from them. You have to ask, "Why? Why would Satan want me to stop being in agreement with this person?"

Of course, there are some people you need to step away from, but most disagreements happen with people you love, and the enemy is working overtime to cause chaos. He loves nothing more than to cause a split (division) between friends and loved ones. Keep that in mind the next time you're in a disagreement. Is it really worth separating friends? Probably not.

Lord, I'll do my best to agree more than I disagree. I see now what the enemy is up to, and I don't want him to divide me from those I care about. Help me, I pray. Amen.

MORE OF HIS UNDERSTANDING

*Trust in the Lord with all your heart,
and do not lean on your own understanding.*
PROVERBS 3:5 ESV

How many times have you mumbled the words, "I just can't figure this out!" Maybe you were working on a math problem at the time. Or maybe you were trying to figure out why a friend suddenly wouldn't speak to you. Perhaps you were trying to figure out why your sister was acting so weird. Life is filled with opportunities to be confused, after all.

It's a good thing to try to understand what's going on, but there are occasions when "figuring it out" isn't possible. In those moments, all you can do is pass it off to the Lord and say, "Father, You figure this one out. It's beyond me."

And here's the good news: He will! He knows what's going on behind the scenes and has every answer to every question.

You were designed to lean on *Him* for understanding, not on yourself. Whew. Doesn't it feel good to know you don't have to figure things out alone? The answers aren't inside of you; they're inside of Him.

Lord, I look to You for answers, not myself. When it comes to the things I can't figure out, teach me to understand Your point of view, Father. Amen.

MORE INDEPENDENT THINKING

Obviously, I'm not trying to win the approval of people, but of God. If pleasing people were my goal, I would not be Christ's servant.
GALATIANS 1:10 NLT

"All the cool kids are doing it."

"Who's going to see you, anyway?"

"What do you mean, you don't drink or smoke?"

"Seriously? You're one of those *Christians*?"

Oh, the things you hear from the kids at school. Sometimes you look around you and wonder if anyone believes in God anymore. Even the ones who claim to be Christians often go along with the crowd and end up in trouble.

The Lord didn't make you to go along with the crowd, girl. You were made for more independent thinking. When they're going north, you go south. When they're going east, you go west. Don't worry about not fitting in. There's only one person you need to fit in with, and that's Jesus. In the end, His opinion is the only one that matters.

So walk away from the crowd-think and get back to Jesus-thinking. Be like Him. Act like Him. Talk like Him. And pretty soon the crowd will be following after you!

I want to be more like You, Jesus. No more going along with the crowd for me. I'm following after You, Lord. Amen.

MORE GODLY COUNSEL

*Plans fail for lack of counsel,
but with many advisers they succeed.*
Proverbs 15:22 niv

Have you ever gone to the wrong friend for advice? People are usually happy to give it, but "godly counsel" needs to line up with the Bible. The Lord wants us to seek out godly advice—people who will speak the Word over us and pray that we make good choices.

So who do you lean on? Do you have a certain friend or teacher you talk to when you have a big decision to make? Are you close enough to one of your parents to get their advice? Do you spend time praying, asking God to give you His perspective?

Here's another question: Are you the sort of friend others come to when they need counsel? Do they see you as wise and caring? God has made you to both give and receive godly counsel. Be available to offer a shoulder to a friend who's hurting or to someone who just needs to talk. And remember, God can give you all the guidance you need. If you don't have that special someone in your life to go to, run into God's arms and listen to His still, small voice.

*May I give and receive godly advice
for the rest of my life, Lord. Amen.*

MORE TRUST IN I AM

*God said to Moses, "I AM WHO I AM."
And he said, "Say this to the people
of Israel: 'I AM has sent me to you.'"*
EXODUS 3:14 ESV

Have you ever played the trust game? Here's how it goes: a bunch of friends stand behind you as you are standing. You fall backward, knowing (or trusting) they will catch you. The problem is, sometimes they will. . .and sometimes they won't!

You're still playing that game, but in a different way. How many times have you stumbled and fallen, only to realize that God (the great I Am) was right there, ready to catch you in His arms? Plenty!

You were made to trust Him, girl, even during those seasons when it feels like you're going to tumble and fall. He has never let you down, and you have no reason to think He'll start now. He's the only trustworthy One. "I Am" means He is in your situation, even now, ready to help. So place your trust in Him, girl, not yourself. He's got this.

*Lord, You are the great I Am, the One who is worthy
of my praise! You are present in the very middle
of my circumstances. When I don't know what's
happening, You do. I trust You no matter what! Amen.*

MORE COMFORT FOR THE HURTING

"I will comfort you there in Jerusalem as a mother comforts her child."
Isaiah 66:13 nlt

Talia came by it honestly—the compassion in her heart toward others who were hurting. The elderly woman down the street who lived alone. The little girl whose parents rarely seemed to take the time for her. The boy from her science class who lived in fear. Talia did her best to comfort and console any brokenhearted person who crossed her path. She even blessed some of them with special cards to lift their spirits.

Maybe you're the same. You are filled with compassion for those who need comforting. They touch your heart in ways you simply can't explain. You go out of your way to draw near to those who need your love and empathy. You shower them with unexpected blessings. It feels so good!

That desire to comfort comes straight from the heart of your heavenly Father. He placed it inside of you so that others could sense His love and compassion through you, girl, so keep it up!

Thank You for Your comfort and compassion, Father! May I receive it. . . and give it to anyone in need today. Amen.

MORE CHANGES

For if a man belongs to Christ, he is a new person.
The old life is gone. New life has begun.
2 Corinthians 5:17 nlv

What if life was exactly the same every single day. . .if nothing ever changed?

What if you always wore the same clothes, ate the same meals, talked to the same kids, went to the same places? What if every conversation with your best friend was exactly the same as the conversation from yesterday? What if the lunch lady at school put chicken nuggets on your plate just like yesterday, and the day before that, and the day before that? Wouldn't life be boring?

Thank goodness, life isn't boring! It's filled with changes, but that's part of what makes it exciting. Sometimes the changes seem overwhelming (or even scary), but you can count on God to see you through every one of them. He created you to enjoy (and appreciate) change.

If you never changed, you'd still be in diapers right now. Pause to think about that for a moment! You couldn't walk or talk or take care of yourself.

Change is a good thing, so don't be surprised when it happens. You were made for it, girl!

Lord, I'll do a better job handling change
from now on. Thanks for creating me
to handle it with Your help. Amen.

MORE DIFFERENCE MAKING

Do not let yourselves get tired of doing good. If we do not give up, we will get what is coming to us at the right time.
GALATIANS 6:9 NLV

"You've really got to stop focusing on others and spend more time on yourself," Kendra's best friend said after clucking her tongue. "Do you ever wear makeup anymore? And what's up with those clothes? You're so busy taking care of others that the important stuff doesn't seem to matter to you anymore."

Ouch. Kendra had a hard time swallowing that statement. Maybe you would've had a hard time too. After all, God created us to do good things for others. Helping your elderly parents or grandparents. Caring for that little one who's sick. Feeding the homeless. Volunteering in the nursery at your church. These are all things that help the world become a better place, after all.

Sure, it's important to keep things in balance in your life. Maybe you really do need to pull back a little and wait for a better season. But even while you're waiting, there's plenty of time (and opportunity) to do good things for others.

If you don't. . .who will?

I want to make a difference in my world, Jesus! I know You've created me to do this. Show me when to slow down and when to speed up, I pray. I want to do great things for You. Amen.

MORE LOVE FOR GOD'S CREATION

The heavens are telling of the greatness of God and the great open spaces above show the work of His hands.
PSALM 19:1 NLV

Bright twinkling stars against a dark night sky. Grand, rushing rivers thundering downstream. Jagged mountains covered in fluffy white snow. A beautiful golden sunset disappearing into the western sky. You were made to love all of these and more!

This world is filled with beautiful things, all made by God, and you're crazy about all of them! Colorful parrots flying from branch to branch. Teensy-tiny butterflies peeking out from their cocoons. Newborn kittens with their little eyes tightly closed, snuggled together in their bed. Bright green lizards, changing color to brown when they slither onto the fence. They're all reminders of just how creative and imaginative our God is.

All of creation—from the tiny leapfrog to the brightest star—testifies to the greatness of God. If you ever begin to doubt that God exists, just look around you, girl! It was all made for your enjoyment. And just think—He made you too. . .just the way you are. You are a part of this glorious creation, bringing joy to those around you.

*I love Your creation, Lord.
How marvelous You are! Amen.*

MORE HANGING OUT WITH HIM

"Yes, I am the vine; you are the branches. Those who remain in me, and I in them, will produce much fruit. For apart from me you can do nothing."
JOHN 15:5 NLT

Imagine a fisherman sitting on the edge of a creek. He baits his hook then tosses the line out into the water. Then. . .he waits. And waits. The sun is blazing overhead, but he's not giving up! The fisherman is absolutely sure a fish will come along and nibble at his line. Until that happens, he's content to just sit and rest, no matter the weather.

God created you to be like that fisherman, girl! He wants you to bait your hook with prayer. Toss out your line. Then. . .wait on His response. Storms might come. Winds might howl. But you can remain there, just hanging out with Him, until the answer comes.

Today's verse says, "Apart from me you can do nothing." No wonder He made you for more time with Him!

Lord, I'm not moving. I'm hanging out with You no matter what storms might come. Without You, I can do nothing. With You, I can do anything! Amen.

MORE VISION CHECKS

Trust in the Lord with all your heart; do not depend on your own understanding. Seek his will in all you do, and he will show you which path to take.
Proverbs 3:5–6 nlt

Megan refused to get glasses, even though she knew she needed them. She was just too embarrassed, thinking about what she might look like. Still, it was getting harder and harder to see the math problems on the board. And seeing the clock from the far side of the room? Impossible.

When she attended her kid sister's choir concert and couldn't tell one kiddo from the other, Megan knew the time had come. She went to the eye doctor and ordered those new glasses. They took some getting used to. At first everything was a blurry mess. After she'd spent a few hours breaking them in, the world came into focus. She could hardly believe all the things she'd been missing—the details on the tree leaves. The sharp colors on the TV screen. Wow! What a difference.

God wants you to have vision checks. . .not just with your physical eyes, but with your spiritual ones. He's up to something. Can you see it? If not, maybe it's time to put on your spiritual glasses for a closer look.

You've designed me to see things the way You do, Lord. I'll put on my spiritual glasses and never be blinded again! Amen.

MORE PRESSING ON

I don't mean to say that I have already achieved these things or that I have already reached perfection. But I press on to possess that perfection for which Christ Jesus first possessed me.
PHILIPPIANS 3:12 NLT

In the animated movie *Finding Nemo*, a little fish named Dory becomes friends with another fish, Nemo. Dory is a little scatterbrained. Okay, she's *very* scatterbrained! She can't seem to remember anything from minute to minute. Dory has a motto: "Just keep swimming! Just keep swimming!" Whenever she gets lost or confused, she sings those words aloud: "Just keep swimming! Just keep swimming!"

God made you for more swimming (more pressing on, even when you don't feel like it). When you're overwhelmed or you don't know what to do: "Just keep swimming. Just keep swimming." Press on, girl. Don't give up!

It's not always easy to keep going, especially when you're tired or confused. Maybe you don't feel like going to school today. Maybe you don't feel up to cleaning your room or doing your homework. Maybe you're not in the mood to help Mom out by washing the dishes. But the "Just keep going" motto will give you the courage (and the energy) to get the job done, and that's what's most important.

You made me to keep pressing on, Jesus, so that's what I'm going to do! Amen.

MORE LOOKING FOR THE GOOD

*Look for good and not sin, that you may live.
Then the Lord God of All will be with you,
just as you have said.*
AMOS 5:14 NLV

Are you one of those girls who's always looking for the bad in people? Do you notice their flaws, their mistakes, and their mess-ups instead of the good things they do?

Corrie was like that. After a school band program, she had a lot of not-so-nice things to say. "Man, Heather did a terrible job on her flute solo, didn't she? Why did the music teacher give her a solo, anyway? There are a lot of talented people who could've done better." Corrie just couldn't seem to help herself. She had to make negative comments about everyone. Except herself, of course. She rarely noticed her own flaws.

God created you to look for the good. When you look for it, you will definitely find it. That's what He does when He looks at you, by the way—He sees the good, not the bad. Instead of pointing out your flaws, He looks at you with love in His eyes. Instead of saying, *"What a mess-up she is!"* He says, *"Wow, look how hard she's trying. That's My girl!"*

Be like Jesus. That's how He made you to be.

*Lord, I want to be more like You,
seeing the good in others. Amen.*

MORE SOARING LIKE EAGLES

But those who trust in the Lord will find new strength. They will soar high on wings like eagles. They will run and not grow weary. They will walk and not faint.
Isaiah 40:31 NLT

Have you ever watched a baby bird fly out of its nest for the first time? The mama gently nudges it to the edge of the nest, and then. . .whoosh! Off it goes, soaring through the sky, wings flapping, the rest of the birdie babies cheering it on.

In many ways the faith walk is a bit like that bird taking to flight. You spend more time worrying about hitting the ground than enjoying the view sometimes. But God designed you to soar like an eagle. There should be more cloud surfing than ground hugging.

What areas of your life are shaky right now? Your grades? Friendships? Problems with Mom and Dad? You're like that baby bird, even now, trusting that your wings really do work. They do! They were given to you by your heavenly Father, and He plans for you to soar like an eagle no matter what you're facing. So don't wait, little one. Let's fly!

Lord, I won't sit in the nest any longer. I won't let fear hold me back. I'll trust in You, and I'll soar over my circumstances! Watch me go! Amen.

MORE STRAIGHT ROADS

*The guilty walk a crooked path;
the innocent travel a straight road.*
PROVERBS 21:8 NLT

Has the "road" of your life been straight or crooked? Most people would have to admit that their road looks more like a rabbit trail in the woods, zigzagging all over the place! No matter where you've come from or what you've been through, God wants to give you straight roads to travel. He made you for that, after all! Zigzagging takes a lot of energy, and you usually end up lost in the woods!

So how do you begin to walk a straight path when the one you've been on has been filled with so many twists and turns? Use your spiritual compass. Keep your eyes on Jesus. When you stay focused, you won't be tempted to move to the right or the left every time a little temptation comes along.

Remember, He's the One leading the way. Follow Him, and He'll straighten out every crooked path.

*Lord, I want to walk a straight path.
Be my Guide. Straighten out the
crooked places, I pray. Amen.*

THE "MORE" LIFESTYLE

And God is able to bless you abundantly, so that in all things at all times, having all that you need, you will abound in every good work.
2 CORINTHIANS 9:8 NIV

Have you figured it out, sweet girl? God adores you. He thinks you're the cat's meow. And He has so many wonderful things lined up for you. There are places to go, people to see, and things to do. There's more love, more hope, more joy, and more opportunity to experience His goodness as you move forward from here.

It's time to adopt a "more" lifestyle. Live with a sense of expectation. See yourself as a conqueror! Enjoy the possibilities of what's coming around the bend. And remember, His love for you isn't just for a day. . .it's for all eternity. (Can you even imagine what "more" will look like in heaven?)

Thank You for creating me for more, Jesus! It's because of Your great love that I've received so many blessings along life's journey. And I know more are coming, not just here but in heaven. I'm looking forward to that day when we'll see each other face-to-face! Amen.